Que®

Excel for Windows™ Quick Reference

Sharel McVey

Excel for Windows Quick Reference.

Library of Congress Catalog Number: 89-60530

ISBN 0-88022-722-2

94   93   92   91   4   3   2   1

Interpretation of the printing code: the rightmost double-digit number is the year of the book's printing; the rightmost single-digit number is the number of the book's printing. For example, a printing code of 90-4 shows that the fourth printing of the book occurred in 1990.

This book is based on Excel for Windows Version 3.0.

Que Quick Reference Series

The *Que Quick Reference Series* is a portable resource of essential microcomputer knowledge. Whether you are a new or experienced user, you can rely on the high-quality information contained in these convenient guides.

The *Que Quick Reference Series* includes these titles:

1-2-3 Quick Reference
1-2-3 Release 2.2 Quick Reference
1-2-3 Release 3 Quick Reference
1-2-3 Release 3.1 Quick Reference
Allways Quick Reference
Assembly Language Quick Reference
AutoCAD Quick Reference, 2nd Edition
C Quick Reference
CorelDRAW Quick Reference
dBASE IV Quick Reference
DOS and BIOS Functions Quick Reference
Excel Quick Reference
Excel for Windows Quick References
Hard Disk Quick Reference
Harvard Graphics Quick Reference
MS-DOS Quick Reference
MS-DOS 5 Quick Reference
Microsoft Word 5.5 Quick Reference
Microsoft Works Quick Reference
Norton Utilities Quick Reference
PC Tools Quick Reference, 2nd Edition
Q&A Quick Reference
Quattro Pro Quick Reference
QuickBASIC Quick Reference
Turbo Pascal Quick Reference
UNIX Programmer's Quick Reference
UNIX Shell Commands Quick Reference
Windows 3 Quick Reference
WordPerfect Quick Reference
WordPerfect 5.1 Quick Reference

iv

Publisher
Lloyd J. Short

Series Product Director
Karen A. Bluestein

Production Editor
Cheryl S. Robinson

Editor
Laura Wirthlin

Technical Editor
Steve Sogge

Production Team
Jill Bomaster
Brad Chinn
Scott Cook
Betty Kish
Bob LaRoche
Kim Leslie
Joe Ramon

Trademark Acknowledgments

1-2-3 is a registered trademark of Lotus Corporation.

dBASE is a registered trademark of Ashton-Tate.

Macintosh is a registered trademark of Apple Computer, Inc.

Microsoft, Microsoft Excel, Microsoft Windows, MS-DOS, and Multiplan are registered trademarks of Microsoft Corporation.

Table of Contents

Introduction

Excel for Windows Quick Reference is not a rehash of
traditional documentation. Instead, this quick reference
is a compilation of the most frequently used information
from Que's best-selling Excel books.

Excel for Windows Quick Reference gives you essential
information on Excel commands, functions, and macros.
You learn the proper use of primary Excel functions, as
well as how to avoid serious errors. This book contains
fundamental information in a compact, easy-to-use
format, but is not intended as a replacement for the
comprehensive information presented in a full-size
guide.

Excel for Windows Quick Reference is divided into
sections. The Command Reference is an alphabetical
listing of Excel commands. Each command is presented
in the same format. Each entry lists the command's
purpose, provides step-by-step instructions for its use,
and gives you further notes or cautions.

Following the Command Reference are sections on
Worksheet Functions, Macros Functions, and Macro
Key Codes.

Now you can put essential information at your fingertips
with *Excel for Windows Quick Reference*—and the
entire *Que Quick Reference Series*!

AN EXCEL OVERVIEW

You can use Microsoft Excel to perform calculations, analyze data, create databases, access external databases, chart data and create graphics, perform "what if" analysis, outline worksheets, and automate routine tasks with macros.

You can use Excel commands for functions such as copying or moving portions of a worksheet, formatting cells to display currency, and using the database. You access Excel commands through a variety of menus.

Choosing Menus and Commands

The *menu bar*, the second line in the worksheet window, shows the menu selections. You can choose a menu item using the keyboard or the mouse.

To choose a menu item using the keyboard

1. Press **Alt** to activate the menu bar.

2. Press the underlined letter (in upper- or lowercase) for the menu you want to see.

   In this book, the keys you press appear in blue.

3. Press the underlined letter of the command you want to use.

   Commands that are not available for selection are dimmed.

To choose a menu item using the mouse

1. Move the pointer to the menu you want to see.

2. Click the menu.

3. Move the pointer to the command you want to use.

   Commands that are not available for selection are dimmed.

4. Click to select the command.

If the command name is followed by an ellipsis (...), a
dialog box prompts you for more information.

Using Dialog Boxes

Dialog boxes can consist of up to six of the following
elements:

- A *list box* is a rectangular area that displays a list of
  choices.

- A *text box* is a rectangular area where you can enter
  relevant text or numbers.

- A *check box* is a small square box used to turn on or
  off a particular option.

- An *option button* is a small round button used to turn
  on one of a group of options.

- A *command button* is a rounded rectangular button
  labeled with a particular action.

- A *drop-down list* is a small rectangular area that
  displays one item in the list and has a down arrow on
  the right that is used to display the complete list of
  choices.

Using the keyboard, you can move around a dialog box
by pressing Tab to go forward and Shift-Tab to go
backward. To select a dialog box option, press Alt and
the underlined letter or number for the option.

Using the mouse, move the pointer to the option and
click.

Pressing the space bar or selecting the default command
button turns on or off an active check box. Pressing
Enter also selects the active command button because
this button contains the command OK. Pressing Enter is
usually the fastest way to accept the dialog box settings,
close the dialog box, and execute the command. Pressing
Esc always selects the Cancel command button, which
usually cancels your dialog box settings and closes the
dialog box.

Navigating

To move to a cell using the mouse, move the pointer to the cell you want to select and click. If the cell is not on-screen, first use the scroll bars to locate and display the cell.

To move to a cell using the keyboard, use the following key(s). A hyphen (-) indicates that you must press the keys at the same time.

Key(s)	Function
←	Moves active cell left one cell.
→	Moves active cell right one cell.
↑	Moves active cell up one cell.
↓	Moves active cell down one cell.
Home	Moves active cell to the beginning of the current row.
End	Moves active cell to the end of the current row.
Home	If Scroll Lock is on, moves active cell to the upper left corner of the window.
End	If Scroll Lock is on, moves active cell to the lower right corner of the window.
PgUp	Moves active cell up one screen.
PgDn	Moves active cell down one screen.
Ctrl-PgUp	Moves active cell left one screen.
Ctrl-PgDn	Moves active cell right one screen.
Ctrl-Home	Moves active cell to cell A1 of the current worksheet.

Ctrl-End	Moves active cell to the last cell of the current worksheet.
Ctrl-←	Moves active cell left to the next intersection of a blank cell and a cell that contains data.
Ctrl-→	Moves active cell right to the next intersection of a blank cell and a cell that contains data.
Ctrl-↑	Moves active cell up to the next intersection of a blank cell and a cell that contains data.
Ctrl-↓	Moves active cell down to the next intersection of a blank cell and a cell that contains data.
F5 (GoTo)	Prompts for a cell reference, range, or range name. After you enter the information and press **Enter**, activates that reference.
Alt,W, window#	Moves active cell to the window whose number you specify.

Many of the basic movement keys also move the cursor in the formula bar while in EDIT mode.

Selecting

Some commands require that you select a cell, a range, multiple areas, a chart object, or another item.

To select an item with the mouse, click on that item. To select adjacent items, click on the first item and drag to highlight the other items. To select nonadjacent items, press and hold the **Ctrl** key while selecting.

To select items with the keyboard, use the following keys:

Key(s)	*Function*
Shift-	Selects as you move. Combine **Shift** with any of the movement keys.
Shift-space bar	Selects the entire row.
Ctrl-space bar	Selects the entire column.
Shift-Ctrl-space bar	Selects the entire worksheet.
F8 (Extend)	Extends the selection as you move (as if you were pressing **Shift**) and anchors the corner cell of the selection. To end Extend mode, press **F8** again.
Shift-F8 (Add)	Adds a nonadjacent area to the current selection. To end Add mode, press **Shift-F8** again.
F5 (GoTo)	Prompts for a cell reference, range, or range name. After you enter the information and press **Enter**, activates the reference.
F8, **F5**	Extends a selection from the active cell to the cell you move to using **F5**.

Moving Within a Selection

Using the cursor-movement keys within a selection unselects the item. To move within a selection, use the following keys:

Key(s)	*Function*
Tab	Moves active cell right one cell.
Shift-Tab	Moves active cell left one cell.
Enter	Moves active cell down one cell.
Shift-Enter	Moves active cell up one cell.
Ctrl-Tab	Moves active cell to the next selected range.
Shift-Ctrl-Tab	Moves active cell to the preceding selected range.

Using Function Keys

Function keys save time when you edit cells, move between windows, save files, and get help. Your keyboard contains 10 or 12 function keys (F1 through F10 or F12). Excel supports all 12 keys, but **Alt-F1** duplicates **F11** and **Alt-F2** duplicates **F12**.

Following is a list of function key combinations and their command equivalents:

Key(s)	*Command*
F1	Help
Shift-F1	Context-sensitive Help
Alt-F1	File New (Chart)
Alt-Shift-F1	File New (Worksheet)
Alt-Ctrl-F1	File New (Macro sheet)
F2	Edit formula in formula bar
Shift-F2	FoRmula Note
Ctrl-F2	Window Show Info

Key(s)	Command
Alt-F2	File Save AS
Alt-Shift-F2	File Save
Alt-Ctrl-F2	File Open
Alt-Ctrl-Shift-F2	File Print
F3	FoRmula Paste Name
Shift-F3	FoRmula PasTe Function
Ctrl-F3	FoRmula Define Name
Ctrl-Shift-F3	FoRmula Create Names
F4	FoRmula Reference
Ctrl-F4	Control Close (document window)
Alt-F4	Control Close (application window) or File EXit
F5	FoRmula Goto
Shift-F5	FoRmula Find (cell contents)
Ctrl-F5	Control Restore (document window)
F6	Next Pane
Shift-F6	Previous Pane
Ctrl-F6	Control Next Window
Ctrl-Shift-F6	Previous document window
F7	FoRmula Find (next occurrence)
Shift-F7	FoRmula Find (previous occurrence)
Ctrl-F7	Control Move (document window)

Key(s)	*Command*
F8	Extend mode (on/off)
Shift-F8	Add mode (on/off)
Ctrl-F8	Control Size (document window)
F9	Options Calculate Now
Shift-F9	Options Calculate DocumeNt
F10	Activate menu bar
Ctrl-F10	Control MaXimize (document window)
F11	File New
Shift-F11	File New (worksheet)
Ctrl-F11	File New (macro sheet)
F12	File Save As
Shift-F12	File Save
Ctrl-F12	File Open
Ctrl-Shift-F12	File Print

═ Tool Bar ═══════════════════════

The *tool bar* displays buttons used for applying styles, creating an outline, selecting all visible cells, summing numbers in a range, formatting and aligning cells, selecting objects, drawing, creating a chart on a worksheet, and creating a picture of a worksheet or macro sheet.

To turn the tool bar on or off, follow these steps:

1. Press **Alt**, **O**, **W** or click the **O**ptions menu and select **W**orkspace.

2. Press **Alt-T** or click the **T**ool Bar check box in the Display area.

The following list describes the tools on the tool bar:

Tool	*Purpose*
Style box	Defines and applies formatting styles.
Promote and demote buttons	Promotes and demotes sections of a worksheet to create an outline.
Show outline symbols	Turns on or off outline symbols. Available only when a worksheet is outlined.
Select visible cells button	Selects all cells on a worksheet or macro sheet that are not hidden.
Auto-sum button	Inserts sum function into the active cell and sums the range of numbers directly above or to the left of the active cell.
Bold and italic buttons	Turns on or off bold or italic formatting
Alignment buttons	Left-aligns, centers, or right-aligns active cell contents or text box.
Selection tool	Selects graphic objects for moving, sizing, formatting, or grouping.
Drawing tools	Creates straight lines, squares, rectangles, ovals, circles, and arcs.
Chart tool	Creates a chart of selected data and displays the chart as a graphic object on a worksheet.

Tool	Purpose
Text tool	On a worksheet or macro sheet, draws a text box that can be moved, resized, and formatted.
Button tool	Draws a button that can be linked to a macro; when you click the button, the macro runs.
Camera tool	Creates a linked picture of a range and pastes it onto a worksheet as an object that can be moved, sized, and formatted.

COMMAND REFERENCE

The command reference is an alphabetical listing of all Microsoft Excel commands. The command name is followed by the purpose of the command and instructions for its use.

Chart Add (Delete) Arrow

Purpose

Adds (or deletes) an arrow on a chart. Used to add (or delete) arrows of various sizes, colors, weights, and styles.

To add an arrow

1. Press **Alt**, **C**, **R** or click the **C**hart menu and select Add A**R**row.

2. Move the arrow with the Forma**T** Mo**V**e command or mouse.

3. Resize the arrow with the Forma**T** Si**Z**e command or mouse.

4. Format the arrow with the FormaT Patterns command or double-click the arrow to display the Patterns dialog box.

To delete an arrow

1. Select the arrow.

2. Press Alt, C, R or click the Chart menu and select Delete ARrow.

Chart Add (Delete) Legend

Purpose

Adds (or deletes) a legend on a chart. A legend identifies the different data series in the chart.

To add a legend

1. Press Alt, C, L or click the Chart menu and select Add Legend.

   The legend appears on the right side of the chart. Excel resizes the plot area to make room for the legend.

2. Move the legend with the FormaT Legend or FormaT Move commands or by dragging with the mouse.

3. Format the legend with the FormaT Patterns command or double-click the legend to display the Patterns dialog box.

To delete the legend

Press Alt, C, L or click the Chart menu and select Delete Legend.

Excel resizes the plot area to fill the extra space.

Chart Add (Delete) Overlay

Purpose

Overlays (or deletes) a second chart over the current
(main) chart to create a combination chart. The data
series are evenly divided between the main chart and
the overlay chart. If the number of data series is odd,
the main chart includes the extra data series.

To add an overlay

1. Press Alt, C, O or click the Chart menu and select
   Add Overlay.

2. Change the overlay chart's type and format with the
   FormaT Overlay command.

To delete the overlay

Press Alt, C, O or click the Chart menu and select
Delete Overlay.

All data series are incorporated in the main chart.

Chart Attach Text

Purpose

Inserts text near a chart object, such as the title, an axis,
a data series, or an overlay.

To attach text

1. Press Alt, C, T or click the Chart menu and select
   Attach Text.

2. Select Chart Title, Value Axis, Category Axis, or
   Series or Data Point.

3. Press Enter or click OK.

4. In the formula bar, type the text you want to attach and press **Enter**.

5. Select Forma**T** **T**ext to format the text or double-click the text (or select Forma**T** **P**atterns) to display the **P**atterns dialog box.

To edit attached text

1. Select the text.

   The text appears in the formula bar.

2. Press **F2** or click the formula bar. Edit the text.

To add unattached text

1. Make sure that no object is selected and the formula bar is blank.

2. In the formula bar, type the text you want to add and press **Enter**.

   The text appears in the center of the chart surrounded by black squares. To move the text with the mouse, click and drag the black squares; with the keyboard, use the Forma**T** **M**ove command.

Chart Axes

Purpose

Hides or displays the category (X) and value (Y) axes.

To hide or display Axes

1. Press **Alt**, **C**, **X** or click the **C**hart menu and select Chart A**X**es.

2. From the dialog box, select the axes you want to hide or display.

3. Press **Enter** or click OK.

Chart Calculate Now

Purpose

When manual calculation is on, recalculates all open worksheets, and then redraws all open charts supported by those worksheets.

To recalculate

Press **Alt, C, N** or press **F9** or click the Chart menu and select Calculate Now. (The worksheets supporting the charts must be open.)

Chart Color Palette

Purpose

Customizes colors in the color palette and copies color palettes between open documents.

To change a color

1. Press **Alt, C, E** or click the Chart menu and select Color PalEtte.

2. Select a color in the palette and select the Edit command. Select another color to replace the color in the palette. Press **Enter** or click OK.

To copy a color palette

1. Press **Alt, C, E** or click the Chart menu and select Color PalEtte.

2. Press **Alt-C** or click the Copy Colors From arrow to see all open documents.

3. To copy the color palette from an open document, select the document name. Press **Enter** or click OK.

To reset the color palette

The Default button in the Color PalEtte dialog box resets the color palette to its original 16 colors.

Chart Edit Series

Purpose

Creates, edits, or deletes a data series on an active chart.

To create, edit, or delete data series

1. Press Alt, C, S or click the Chart menu and select Edit Series.

2. Select the data series you want to edit or delete from the Series box. Select New Series to create a new data series.

3. Press Alt-E or click the DElete button to delete the selected data series.

4. Edit the formulas in the Name, X Labels, or Y Values text boxes. Press Alt-D or click the Define button to plot the data series on the active chart.

5. Use Plot Order to define the order in which the selected data series is plotted on the chart. (You can plot up to 255 series.)

6. Press Enter or click OK to accept the changes and close the dialog box.

Chart Full (Short) Menus

Purpose

Full menus sets all menus to display all options. Short menus sets all menus to display only the most-used options, which speeds command selection and makes Excel simpler for new users.

To display full menus

Press Alt, C, M or click the Chart menu and select Full Menus.

To display short menus

Press Alt, C, M or click the Chart menu and select Short Menus.

Chart Gridlines

Purpose

Displays or hides major and minor gridlines attached to the category and value axes.

To display or hide gridlines

1. Press Alt, C, G or click the Chart menu and select Gridlines.

2. Set Category Axis Major Gridlines, Category Axis MInor Gridlines, Value Axis MajOr Gridlines, and Value Axis MiNor Gridlines.

3. Press Enter or click OK.

Chart Protect (Unprotect) Document

Purpose

Protects (or unprotects) a chart's data series, formats, and window from change. Provides password protection.

To protect a chart

1. Press Alt, C, P or click the Chart menu and select Protect Document.

2. Turn on Chart to protect the chart's data series and formats.

3. Turn on Windows to protect the chart's window screen position, size, and other characteristics.

4. Select Password and enter a password.

5. Press Enter or click OK.

To unprotect a chart

1. Press **Alt**, **C**, **P** or click the **C**hart menu and select Un**P**rotect Document.

   If you did not password-protect the chart, you can alter the chart. If you did password-protect the chart, you must supply the password to alter the chart.

2. Type the password and press **Enter** or click OK.

   If you do not enter the correct password, Excel beeps and displays an error message. Repeat Step 2.

Chart Select Chart

Purpose

Selects all elements of a chart, enabling **E**dit commands to affect all aspects of the chart.

To select an entire chart

1. Press **Alt**, **C**, **C** or click the **C**hart menu and choose the Select Chart command

2. Use the **E**dit ClE**a**r command to delete the chart's data series or formats.

3. Use the **E**dit **C**opy command to copy the chart's data series or formats to the clipboard.

4. To unselect the chart, press **Esc** or an arrow key or click the mouse.

Chart Select Plot Area

Purpose

Selects a chart's plot area, enabling Forma**T** **P**atterns setting changes to affect all elements in the area bounded by the axes.

To select the plot area

1. Press **Alt, C, A** or click the **C**hart menu and select Plot **A**rea.

2. Use the Forma**T P**atterns command to change the border style, border color, border weight, background pattern, background color, or foreground color of the plot area.

3. To unselect the chart, press an arrow key or click the mouse.

═ Control Close

Purpose

Closes the active application or document window.

To close an application window

Press **Alt, space bar, C** or press **Alt-F4** or click the Application Control menu and select **C**lose.

To close a document window

Press **Alt, -, C** or press **Ctrl-F4** or click the Document Control menu and select **C**lose.

═ Control Maximize

Purpose

Expands the active application or document window to fill the screen space.

To expand an application window

Press **Alt, space bar, X** or click the Application Control menu and select Ma**X**imize; or click the maximize icon in the upper right corner of the application window.

To expand a document window

Press **Alt**, **-**, **X** or press **Ctrl-F10** or click the Document Control menu and select MaXimize or click the maximize icon in the upper right corner of the document window.

To restore a window

Control **R**estore returns the window to its preceding size and location.

Control Minimize

Purpose

Provides more on-screen space by collapsing the active application window to an icon at the bottom of the screen.

To collapse an application window

Press **Alt**, **space bar**, **N** or click the Application Control menu and select MiNimize or click the minimize icon in the upper right corner of the application window.

To restore an application window

Control **R**estore returns the window to its preceding size and location.

Control Move

Purpose

Moves the active application or document window. The Control **M**ove command is available only when the window is in the restored position.

To move an application window with the keyboard

1. Press **Alt**, **space bar**, **M** or click the Application Control menu and select Move.

2. Press the arrow keys to move the window. Press **Ctrl** while pressing the arrow keys to move in smaller increments.

3. After you position the window, press **Enter**.

To move a document window with the keyboard

1. Press **Alt**, **-**, **M** or press **Ctrl-F7** or click the Document Control menu and select **M**ove.

2. Press the arrow keys to move the window. Press **Ctrl** while pressing the arrow keys to move in smaller increments.

3. After you position the window, press **Enter**.

To move a window with the mouse

Move the window by dragging its title bar.

═ **Control Next Window** ═

Purpose

Switches to the next open document window.

To switch to the next window

Press **Alt**, **-**, **N** or press **Ctrl-F6** or click the Document Control menu and select **N**ext Window.

═ **Control Restore** ═

Purpose

Restores an application or document window to its preceding size and location, but does not affect changes made by the Control Size and Control Move commands.

To restore an application window

Press **Alt**, **space bar**, **R** or click the Application Control menu and select **R**estore or click the restore icon in the upper right corner of the application window.

To restore a document window

Press **Alt**, **-**, **R** or press **Ctrl-F5** or click the Document Control menu and select **R**estore or click the restore icon in the upper right corner of the document.

Control Run

Purpose

Runs the **C**lipboard, the Control **P**anel, the **M**acro Translator, or the **D**ialog Editor.

To operate these features

1. Press **Alt**, **space bar**, **U** or click the Application Control menu and select **RU**n.

2. Select the **C**lipboard to see the contents, the Control **P**anel to adjust system settings, the **M**acro Translator to convert Lotus 1-2-3 macros to Excel macros, or the **D**ialog Editor to create custom dialog boxes.

3. Press **Enter** or click OK.

Control Size

Purpose

Changes the size of the active application or document window. This command is available only when the window is in the restored position.

To change the size of an application window with the keyboard

1. Press **Alt, space bar, S** or click the Application Control menu and select **S**ize.

2. Press the arrow keys to resize the window. To resize the window in smaller increments, press **Ctrl** and the appropriate arrow key.

3. When the window is the desired size, press **Enter**.

To change the size of a document window with the keyboard

1. Press **Alt, -, S** or press **Ctrl-F8** or click the Document Control menu and select **S**ize.

2. Press the arrow keys to resize the window. To resize the window in smaller increments, press **Ctrl** and the appropriate arrow key.

3. When the window is the desired size, press **Enter**.

To change the size of a window with the mouse

Resize a window by dragging the window border. The mouse pointer changes shape when positioned on the window border.

═║ **Control Split** ║════════════════════

Purpose

Divides the active document window into panes and creates separate scrolls for each pane. This command is available only for worksheets and macro sheets.

To divide the document window with the keyboard

1. Press **Alt, -, T** or click the Document Control menu and select Spli**T**.

2. Press the arrow keys to move the split panes pointer until you have the desired division.

3. Press **Enter**.

To divide the document window with the mouse

Drag the split bars from the solid black rectangles that appear next to the scroll arrows (at the window's bottom left and top right corners). The mouse pointer changes shape while on the split bars.

Control Switch To

Purpose

Displays the Task List and all open applications. Enables you to switch to another open application.

To switch to another application

1. Press **Alt**, **space bar**, **W** or click the Application Control menu and select S**W**itch To or press **Ctrl-Esc** to display the Task List dialog box.

2. Select from the list the open application to which you want to switch.

3. Press **Alt-S** or click the **S**witch button.

Data Consolidate

Purpose

Consolidates data from multiple ranges or multiple worksheets into a single range.

To consolidate data

1. Select the destination area for the consolidated data. The destination area can be a single cell, a range of cells, a single column, or a single row.

2. Press **Alt**, **D**, **N** or click the **D**ata menu and select Co**N**solidate.

3. Select the function you want to use to consolidate data. The default function is SUM.

4. Select the Top Row and Left Column check boxes if you want to consolidate data by category labels. (If a category check box is turned off, that data is consolidated by position.)

5. Press Alt-R or click the Reference text box.

6. Select the data you want to consolidate.

7. Press Alt-A or click the Add button to add a range to the All References list. You can specify up to 255 ranges. To delete a reference, select the reference from the All REferences list and press Alt-D or click the Delete button.

8. Press Alt-S or click the Create Link to Source Data check box if you want Excel to update the data in the destination area when the source data changes.

9. Press Enter or click OK to consolidate data. Press Alt-F4 or click the Close button to close the CoNsolidate dialog box without consolidating data.

Data Delete

Purpose

Erases database records that match the criteria in the criteria range, and moves subsequent records to fill the empty space. This command has no effect on worksheet data outside the database.

To delete specified data

1. Define your database range and criteria range using the Data Set DataBase and Data Set Criteria commands.

2. Enter your criteria.

3. Preview the data you want to delete using the Data Find or Data Extract command.

4. Press Alt, D, D or click the Data menu and select Delete.

Caution

Because you cannot undo the effects of the Data Delete command, be careful what you specify for elimination. Do not include blank rows in the criteria range because the command then matches and deletes all records in the database.

Data Extract

Purpose

Copies database records that match specified criteria into the extract range.

To extract data

1. Define your database range, criteria range, and extract range using the Data Set DataBase, Data Set Criteria, and Data Set EXtract commands.

2. Enter your criteria.

3. Select the range of cells that you want to hold the extracted data. The first row of the range must contain the names of the database fields with which you want to work.

   If you select the first row and any rows below the first row, the extracted data is limited to those rows only and clears those cells of data. Excel copies as much data as space permits and then displays a message warning that the extract range is full.

   If you select the first row only, the extract range is unlimited and all cells below are defined as part of the extract range. The cells are cleared of data, however, whether data copies to them or not.

4. Press Alt, D, E or click the Data menu and select the Extract command.

5. Select whether to extract Unique Records Only. This setting filters out duplicate database records.

6. Press Enter or click OK.

The records matching your criteria copy to the extract range. Excel extracts only the value of the formula from a record containing a formula.

Caution

Because you cannot reverse the clearing of cell contents with Edit Undo, use the extract command with caution.

Data Find (Exit Find)

Purpose

Selects records in the database that match the criteria in your criteria range. Data Exit Find exits the Find mode.

To find data

1. Define your database range and criteria range using the Data Set DataBase Data and Set Criteria commands.

2. Enter your criteria. One of the following operators must precede the criteria: =, >, <, >=, <=, or < >.

3. Press Alt, D, F or click the Data menu and select Find. For a backward search, press Shift as you select Find.

   If the active cell is outside the database when you execute the command, Excel selects the first record that matches the criteria. If the active cell is in the database, Excel selects the first record that matches the criteria after the active cell.

4. Move across fields in the selected record by pressing Tab or Enter to go right, Shift-Tab or Shift-Enter to go left.

5. Move to the next or preceding matching record by pressing the down- or up-arrow key or clicking the down or up scroll arrow.

   Excel beeps when it finds no more matches.

6. Move to the next or preceding matching record that is at least a page away by pressing **PgDn** or **PgUp** or by clicking below or above the scroll box.

   Excel beeps when it finds no more matches.

7. Scroll the screen the length of the database by pressing the right- or left-arrow key or by dragging the scroll box.

8. After examining the matching records, press **Esc** or select the **D**ata Exit **F**ind command or click a cell outside the database.

To exit the Find mode

Press **Alt**, **D**, **F** or press **Esc** or click the **D**ata menu and select Exit **F**ind. The scroll bars return to normal.

Data Form

Purpose

Enables you to view, find, edit, add, and delete database records, offering an alternative to many of the **D**ata menu commands.

To access the database form

1. Define your database range using the **D**ata Set Data**B**ase command.

2. Press **Alt**, **D**, **O**, or click the **D**ata menu and select F**O**rm.

   The left side of the dialog box contains a list of all database field names. To the right of each field name is the field's entry for the first record. To the right of the record entries are the command buttons.

3. To move among entries, use the following keys:

Key	Action
Tab	Moves forward among record entries and command buttons.
Shift-Tab	Moves backwards among record entries and command buttons.
Enter	Moves to the top of the next record.
Shift-Enter	Moves to the top of the preceding record.
Ctrl-PgUp	Moves to the first record in the database.
Ctrl-PgDn	Moves to the end of the database and creates a new record.
Down-arrow	Moves to the same field in the next record.
Up-arrow	Moves to the same field in the preceding record.

To add new records

1. Access the database form.
2. Select NeW or press Ctrl-PgDn or click and drag the scroll box to the bottom of the scroll bar.
3. Enter new data in the appropriate fields.
4. Move to the next empty record by pressing Enter.
5. Press Alt-F4 or click CLose.

To remove a record

1. Access the database form.
2. Select the record.
3. Select Delete and press Enter or click OK.

   The record is permanently deleted, and Excel renumbers all subsequent records.
4. Press Alt-F4 or click CLose.

To change a field entry

1. Access the database form.

2. Select and edit the database field.

3. Press **Alt-F4** or click **CL**ose.

To find specific records

1. Access the database form.

2. Select **C**riteria to display criteria options.

3. Select **C**lear to remove preceding criteria entries.

4. Enter criteria for the appropriate field(s). Precede the criteria with one of the following operators: =, >, <, >=, <=, or <>. If you omit the operator, Excel uses =.

   This criteria is separate from the criteria range, which **D**ata F**O**rm ignores.

5. Press **Enter** to find the first matching record.

6. Select Find **N**ext to display the next matching record or Find **P**rev to find the preceding matching record.

7. Press **Alt-F4** or click CL**ose**.

Data Parse

Purpose

Distributes imported cell contents across multiple columns (typically the result of importing data from another application).

To distribute data across columns

1. Select cells that contain multiple data.

2. Press **Alt**, **D**, **P** or click the **D**ata menu and select **P**arse.

   The data in the first cell of your selected range appears on the **P**arse Line.

3. Select **C**lear to clear the brackets indicating where the data is split into separate columns.

4. Select **G**uess to have Excel insert brackets in suggested places to split the data.

5. Edit the **P**arse Line by inserting and deleting brackets.

6. Press **Enter** or click OK.

    Selected cells are parsed based on the bracket placements in the first cell.

Data Series

Purpose

Fills the selected range with a series of numbers or dates based on the value in the first cell and your command settings.

To fill a range with a series of numbers or dates

1. Enter starting values in the first row or column of the range.

2. Select the range.

3. Press **Alt**, **D**, **R** or click the **D**ata menu and select Se**R**ies.

4. Select whether to fill the range based on the starting values in its **R**ows or **C**olumns.

5. Enter the **S**tep Value, the amount by which each successive cell in the range increases.

6. Select **L**inear to add the **S**tep Value to each successive cell, **G**rowth to multiply the **S**tep Value by each successive cell, or **D**ate to generate a series of numeric dates.

7. If you select **D**ate, also select whether you want the dates to progress by D**A**y, **W**eekday, **M**onth, or **Y**ear.

8. Enter a St**O**p Value to set a number-generation ceiling, unless you want to generate numbers to the end of the range.

9. Press **Enter** or click OK.

Data Set Criteria

Purpose

Defines the range of cells containing the database criteria.

To define criteria

1. Select a range of cells to hold the database criteria. Place the criteria range just above the database to keep the criteria in view.

    The range must be at least two rows. The first row contains the names of the database fields and the following row(s) contain the criteria.

    Precede the criteria with one of the following operators: =, >, <, >=, <=, or <>. If you omit the operator, Excel uses =.

2. Press **Alt**, **D**, **C**, or click the **D**ata menu and select Set **C**riteria.

    Excel defines the criteria range, and names the range Criteria.

    You can define only one criteria range at a time in a worksheet; however, you can set up multiple ranges in the criteria format, then use this command to assign the defined criteria to the ranges.

Data Set Database

Purpose

Defines the range of cells comprising the database.

To define a database

1. Select a range of cells to hold the database. Place the database just below the criteria range to keep the criteria in view.

The cells can be blank or nonblank. The range must be at least three rows. The first row must contain the field names. The following rows contain database records and a blank row.

A database can be as large as the entire worksheet (256 fields and 16,383 records), but you do not need to select all rows when you define the database. As long as your range includes a blank last row, the database range redefines as it grows.

2. Press Alt, D, B or click the Data menu and select Set DataBase.

    Excel defines the database, and names the range Database.

    You can define only one database at a time in a worksheet; however, you can define multiple range names in the database, then use the Data Set DataBase command to assign the database definition to the named ranges.

Data Set Extract

Purpose

Defines the selected cells as the extract range for copying records that match the criteria.

To define an extract range

1. Select a range of cells to hold the copied records that match the criteria defined in the criteria range.

    The extract range must be outside your database and can contain only field names or field names and the selected cells below the field names that will contain the copied data.

    If you select the first row and any rows below the first row, the extracted data is limited to those rows only and clears those rows of data. Excel copies as much data as space permits and then displays a message warning that the extract range is full.

If you select only the first row of field names, the extract range is unlimited and all cells below are defined as part of the extract range. The cells are cleared of data, however,whether data copies to them or not. You cannot reverse this clearing with **E**dit **U**ndo, so use this command with caution.

2. Press **Alt**, **D**, **X** or click the **D**ata menu and select Set E**X**tract.

   Excel defines the extract range and names the range Extract. (You do not have to define an extract range to extract database records. You can select an extract range before selecting the **D**ata **E**xtract command.)

3. Select whether to extract **U**nique Records Only.

   This setting filters out duplicate database records.

4. Press **Enter** or click OK.

   The records matching your criteria are copied to the extract range. Excel extracts only the value of a formula from a record containing a formula.

Data Sort

Purpose

Organizes selected records based on a sort key row or column.

To sort data

1. Define your database range using the **D**ata Set Data**B**ase command.

2. Select the database records that you want to sort. (Do not include the field names.)

3. Press **Alt**, **D**, **S**, or click the **D**ata menu and select **S**ort.

4. Select whether you want to sort by **R**ows or by **C**olumns.

5. Enter the 1st Key sort. If you selected **R**ows in
    Step 4, specify a column by which you want to sort.
    If you selected **C**olumns in Step 4, specify a row by
    which you want to sort.

6. Select whether to sort by **A**scending or **D**escending
    order.

7. If necessary, enter other sort keys and repeat Steps 5
    and 6.

8. Press **Enter** or click OK.

Data Table

Purpose

Substitutes values from a selected range for the value in
a specified cell, then generates a "what if " table of the
results from a specified formula or formulas.

To create a single-input table

1. In a single row or single column, create a list of
    values to be substituted for the value in the input cell.

2. If the values are in a column, enter the formula that
    refers to the input cell in the row above the first value
    and one cell to the right of the column of values. If
    the values are in a row, enter the formula in the
    column to the left of the first value and one cell below
    the row of values.

3. Select the rectangular range containing the formula
    and the list of values.

4. Press **Alt**, **D**, **T** or click the **D**ata menu and select
    Table.

5. Enter the cell reference in which you want to
    substitute the list of values. If the values are in a row,
    enter the reference in the **R**ow Input Cell box; if in a
    column, enter the reference in the **C**olumn Input Cell
    box.

6. Press **Enter** or click OK.

To create a two-input table

1. In a cell directly above a column of values and to the left of a row of values, enter the formula that refers to the two input cells.

2. Select the range that includes the formula (in the upper left corner) and the two lists of values.

3. Press **Alt**, **D**, **T** or click the **D**ata menu and select **T**able.

4. Enter the cell references in which you want to substitute the list of values. For values in the row, enter the cell reference in the **R**ow Input Cell box. For values in the column, enter the cell reference in the **C**olumn Input Cell box.

5. Press **Enter** or click OK.

Edit Clear

Purpose

Removes selected cell formulas, formats, notes, and characters from the formula bar, and data series and formats from charts.

To clear a cell or range

1. Activate the cell or range you want to clear.

2. Press **Alt**, **E**, **E** or press **Del** or click the **E**dit menu and select Cl**E**ar.

3. If a dialog box appears, select the button that describes what you want to clear: **A**ll, Forma**T**s, Fo**R**mulas, or **N**otes. Then press **Enter** or click OK.

   For charts, select **S**eries or **F**ormats. Then press **Enter** or click OK.

Cautions

Do not confuse this command with **Edit Delete**, which removes not only a cell's contents and formatting, but also the cell itself.

In formulas, a cleared cell has a value of zero.

Edit Copy

Purpose

Copies a cell, a range of cells, characters from the formula bar, or an entire chart to the Clipboard.

To copy a selection to the Clipboard

1. Select a cell, a range of cells, characters from the formula bar, or an entire chart.

2. Press **Alt**, **E**, **C** or press **Ctrl-Ins**, or click the **E**dit menu and select **C**opy.

   A marquee appears around your selection, and the data and formatting of the selection copies to the Clipboard.

3. Select a single destination cell.

4. To make only one copy, press **Enter**. To make multiple copies, use the **E**dit **P**aste or **E**dit Paste **S**pecial command. Press **Esc** to clear the marquee.

Notes

Excel also provides the following "quick copy" alternatives:

Ctrl-'	Copies formula or text from cell above.
Ctrl-"	Copies value or text from cell above.
Ctrl-Enter	Copies selected data in the formula bar to a selected range, filling the range.

See also **E**dit Fill Do**W**n, **E**dit Fill Left, **E**dit Fill Rig**H**t, and **E**dit Fill Up.

Edit Copy Picture

Purpose

Copies a pictorial representation of the selection to the Clipboard for use in Excel or another application.

To copy a selection to the Clipboard

1. Select the range or chart you want to copy as a picture. (The selection restrictions on Edit Copy do not apply.)

2. Press Alt, Shift-E, C or press Shift, click the Edit menu, and select Copy Picture.

3. Select whether you want the picture's appearance As Shown on Screen or As Shown when Printed.

4. Press Enter or click OK.

5. Select the destination and use the Paste command to insert the picture.

Edit Cut

Purpose

Moves the selected data and formatting to the Clipboard for use in another location. In a chart, the Edit CuT command is available only when characters are selected in the formula bar.

To move a selection to the Clipboard

1. In a worksheet or macro sheet, select a cell, a range of cells, or characters from the formula bar. In a chart, select characters from the formula bar.

2. Press Alt, E, T or press Shift-Del or click the Edit menu and select CuT.

    A marquee appears around the selection and the data and formatting of the selection is copied to the Clipboard.

3. Select a single destination cell and press **Enter** to
    move the selected data and formatting to the new
    destination. (Select a single cell rather than a range in
    order to avoid problems with ranges that are not the
    same in size.)

If you select characters from the formula bar and
select the **Edit CuT** command, the characters are
removed to the Clipboard. Select a single destination
cell and select the **Edit Paste** command. The
characters appear in the selected cell. A copy of the
characters remains on the Clipboard, enabling you to
make multiple copies.

Caution

Do not confuse this command with **Edit Delete** or **Edit
ClEar**, which remove—rather than move—data.

Edit Delete

Purpose

Removes specified cells, rows, or columns (and all
associated data and formatting) from the worksheet,
and shifts the surrounding cells to fill the space.

To delete cells, rows, or columns

1. Select the cells, rows, or columns you want to delete.

2. Press **Alt, E, D**, or press **Ctrl- –** (dash) or click the
    Edit menu and select **Delete**.

3. Select the Shift Cells **L**eft, Shift Cells **U**p, Entire
    Row, or Entire **C**olumn button and press **Enter** or
    click OK.

    Formulas that refer to the deleted cells cannot locate
    these cells and display the error value #REF!.

Note

See also **Edit ClEar**, which removes a cell's data,
formatting, and notes, but leaves the cell in place.

Edit Fill Down (Up)

Purpose

Copies the data and formats of the top (or bottom) of a range into the rest of the range.

To fill a range

1. Select one or more ranges.

2. To Fill DoWn, press **Alt**, **E**, **W** or press **Ctrl-<** or click the **E**dit menu and select Fill DoWn.

   To Fill Up, press **Alt**, **Shift-E**, **W** or press **Shift**, click the **E**dit menu, and select Fill Up (**W**).

   The data and formats of the top (or bottom) of your range(s) copy into the selected cells below (or above) them. The ranges remain selected for further commands.

Notes

This command has no effect on the part of the range you copy, but it erases the destination cells.

See also **E**dit **C**opy.

Edit Fill Right (Left)

Purpose

Copies the data and formats of the right (or left) column of a range into the rest of the range.

To fill a range

1. Select one or more ranges.

2. To Fill RigHt, press **Alt**, **E**, **H** or press **Ctrl->** or click the **E**dit menu and select Fill RigHt.

   To Fill Left, press **Alt**, **Shift-E**, **H**, or press **Shift**, click the **E**dit menu, and select Fill Left (**H**).

The data and formats of the left (or right) column of
your range(s) copy into the selected cells to the right
(or left). The ranges remain selected for further
commands.

Notes

This command has no effect on the part of the range you
copy, but it erases the destination cells.

See also Edit Copy.

Edit Fill Workgroup

Purpose

Copies the contents of the range of cells selected on an
active worksheet to the same range of cells in all other
sheets in the workgroup.

To fill a workgroup

1. Select the Window Workgroup command. Define a
    workgroup by selecting the open worksheets or
    macro sheets that you want to include in the
    workgroup.

2. Select a range in the active worksheet that you
    want to copy to the same range in all sheets in the
    workgroup.

3. Press Alt, E, G or click the Edit menu and select Fill
    WorkGroup.

4. Select the All, FoRmulas, or Formats button to copy
    all data and formats, data only, or formats only.

5. Press Enter or click OK.

Notes

This command has no effect on the range you copy, but
it erases the destination cells.

See also Window Workgroup and Window Arrange
Workgroup.

Edit Insert

Purpose

Inserts a blank cell or range, pushing existing cells to the
right or down. Formulas that refer to the moved cells are
revised to correspond to their new location.

To insert a blank cell or range

1. Select a range the same size as the range you want to
   insert.

2. Press **Alt**, **E**, **I** or press **Ctrl- +** or click the **E**dit menu
   and select **I**nsert.

3. Select the Shift Cells **R**ight, Shift Cells **D**own, Entire
   Row, or Entire **C**olumn button and press **Enter** or
   click OK.

Edit Paste

Purpose

Pastes a copy of the Clipboard's contents in a specific
location. Preceded by Excel's **E**dit commands or a
comparable command from another application.

To paste a selection

1. Use **E**dit **C**opy or **E**dit Cu**T** from within Excel or a
   comparable command from another application to
   insert information on the Clipboard.

2. Select one cell in which you want to paste the copied
   data.

3. Press **Alt**, **E**, **P** or press **Shift-Ins** or click the **E**dit
   menu and select **P**aste. The copy appears in the new
   location.

Edit Paste Link

Purpose

Pastes data with absolute references that refer to a cell or range copied to the Clipboard. A change in the original is mirrored in its copies. Generally preceded by the Edit Copy or Edit CuT command or a comparable command from another application.

To paste and link a selection

1. Use Edit Copy or Edit CuT from within Excel or a comparable command from another application to insert the information on the Clipboard.

2. Select the location in which you want to link the copied data or chart. If the selected range is not as large as the copied range, only the selected cells are filled.

3. Press Alt, E, L or click the Edit menu and select Paste Link.

   Excel inserts the absolute reference formula(s). In most cases (except Edit CuT), you can make multiple copies.

   If you copy more than one cell, the command pastes an array.

Edit Paste Special

Purpose

Pastes data on the Clipboard and offers various pasting options for combining copied data with data in the destination cells. Preceded by the Edit Copy command or a comparable command from another application.

To paste and combine a selection

1. Use the Edit Copy command or a comparable command from another application to insert information on the Clipboard.

2. Select the location where you want to paste the copied data.

3. Press **Alt**, **E**, **S** or click the **E**dit menu and select Paste **S**pecial.

4. A dialog box appears offering the following pasting options: **A**ll, Fo**R**mulas, **V**alues, Forma**T**s, or **N**otes.

5. If you choose **A**ll, Fo**R**mulas, or **V**alues, select how you want to combine the copied data with the destination cells.

   The options are N**O**ne, which replaces the paste area data with the copied data; A**D**d, which adds the copied data to the paste area data; **S**ubtract, which subtracts the copied data from the paste area data; **M**ultiply, which multiplies the copied data and the paste area data; and D**I**vide, which divides the paste area data by the copied data.

6. Turn on Skip **B**lanks to skip copying blank cells from the Clipboard.

7. Turn on Transpos**E** to reorient the copied data.

8. Press **Enter** or click OK.

Notes

Use this command to format new worksheets with cell properties that you created for an existing worksheet.

Use this command to convert formulas to values by copying, selecting the **V**alues option, and then pasting the copies over the formulas.

Edit Repeat

Purpose

Repeats certain Excel operations.

To repeat an operation

1. Perform an Excel operation that **R**epeat can perform.

   The message `Can't Repeat` appears on the **E**dit menu if the operation cannot be performed by **R**epeat.

2. Press **Alt**, **E**, **R**, or press **Alt-Enter** or click the **E**dit menu and select **R**epeat.

You can repeat this operation until you perform a different operation.

Edit Undo

Purpose

Reverses many Excel operations, including entering or editing worksheet data, all **E**dit commands, Fo**R**mula **A**pply Names, Fo**R**mula R**E**place, Forma**T** Justify, **D**ata **P**arse, and **D**ata **S**ort commands. Can undo only the most recent operation.

To reverse an operation

1. Perform an Excel operation that **U**ndo can reverse.

2. Press **Alt**, **E**, **U** or press **Alt-Backspace** or click the **E**dit menu and select **U**ndo.

File Activate File

Purpose

Lists the last four active Excel files and allows you to open them.

To activate a file

1. Press **Alt**, **F**, or click the **F**ile menu to display the last four active Excel files.

2. Open a file by typing the number to the left of the file name or by clicking the file name.

File Close

Purpose

Closes the active document and its window(s).

To close a file

1. Press **Alt**, **F**, **C** or press **Ctrl-F4** or click the **F**ile menu and select **C**lose.

2. If the document has unsaved changes, Excel asks whether you want to save the file. Select **Y**es to save the document and close the window(s), **N**o to abandon your changes and close the window(s), or Cancel (by pressing **Esc** or clicking the Cancel button) to return to the document as if you had not selected the **F**ile **C**lose command.

Caution

Be sure to save documents before closing to avoid losing changes.

File Close All

Purpose

Closes all open documents and their windows.

To close all files

1. Press **Alt**, **Shift-F**, **C** or press **Shift**, click the **F**ile menu, and select **C**lose All.

2. If any document has unsaved changes, Excel asks whether you want to save the file. Select **Y**es to save the document or **N**o to abandon your changes.

   If you select Cancel at any point, no files close and you return to the active document. The files you saved before you selected Cancel remain saved.

Cautions

File EXit performs the File Close All command and exits Excel.

File Delete

Purpose

Permanently deletes a file from disk.

To delete a file

1. Press **Alt**, **F**, **D** or click the **F**ile menu and select **D**elete.

   Files in the current directory appear in the **F**iles list box. Available drives and directories appear in the **D**irectories list box.

   Scroll through the **F**iles list with the scroll bar.

2. Select the file name from the list box or type the name in the File **N**ame text box.

3. Press **Enter** or click OK. Press **Enter** or click Yes to confirm your choice.

4. After deleting files, press **Esc** or click Close to close the **D**elete dialog box.

Caution

You cannot retrieve deleted files.

File Exit

Purpose

Closes open documents and exits Excel.

To close all files and exit Excel

1. Press Alt, F, X or press Alt-F4 or click the File menu and select EXit.

   To close all documents but remain in Excel, select the File Close All command.

2. If any document has unsaved changes, Excel asks whether you want to save the file. Select Yes to save the document or No to abandon your changes.

   If you select Cancel (by pressing Esc or clicking the Cancel button) at any point, the entire operation is canceled. You remain in Excel, no files close, and you return to the active document. The files you saved before you select Cancel remain saved.

File Links

Purpose

Lists the supporting documents of the active linked document and enables you to open any supporting document. You also can switch links to a different document.

To open linked documents

1. Activate the linked document you want to use.

2. Press Alt, F, L or click the File menu and select Links.

   The names of all linked documents appear in the Links list box.

3. Select the file(s) you want to open. To select adjoining files, press the Shift- up- or down-arrow keys. To select nonadjoining files, press the Ctrl- up- or down-arrow keys to move through the list and the space bar to select the files.

4. Turn on the Read Only option if you want only to see and not to change the files.

5. To open the selected file(s), press **Enter** or click **O**pen.

To switch a link to a different document

1. Activate the linked document you want to use.

2. Press **Alt**, **F**, **L** or click the **F**ile menu and select **L**inks.

3. Select the supporting document you want to change and then select **C**hange.

   A second dialog box appears.

4. Select the file from the list or type the name in the **C**opy from file text box, and press **Enter** or click OK.

═ File New ═══════════════════════

Purpose

Creates a new worksheet, chart, or macro sheet in a window. The number of open documents is limited only by your system's memory.

To create a new file

1. Press **Alt**, **F**, **N** or click the **F**ile menu and select **N**ew.

   Excel asks whether you want to create a **W**orksheet, **C**hart, or **M**acro Sheet.

2. Select the type of document you want to create and press **Enter** or click OK.

   The document appears in a new window and is selected.

Note

You also can press **Alt-Shift-F1** or **Shift-F11** to open a new worksheet, **Alt-F1** or **F11** to open a new chart, and **Alt-Ctrl-F1** or **Ctrl-F11** to open a new macro sheet.

File Open

Purpose

Opens an existing file.

To open a file

1. Press **Alt**, **F**, **O** or press **Alt-Ctrl-F2** or press
   Ctrl-F12 or click the **F**ile menu and select **O**pen.

   Files in the current directory appear in the **F**iles list
   box. Available drives and directories appear in the
   Directories box.

   Scroll through the **F**iles list using the scroll bar.

   Turn on the **R**ead Only option if you want only to see
   and not to change the file. (This option is applicable
   to networks, where several people may use the same
   file simultaneously.)

2. Select the file from the **F**iles list box or type its name
   in the File **N**ame box.

3. Press **Enter** or click OK.

Note

In addition to its own Normal format, Excel can open
files in the following formats:

Text	Also called ASCII, a generic PC format.
CSV	Comma Separated Values.
SYLK	Used by other Microsoft worksheets.
WKS	Used by Lotus 1-2-3 Release 1A.
WK1	Used by Lotus 1-2-3 Release 2.
DIF	Data Interchange Format.
DBF 2	Used by dBASE II.

DBF 3   Used by dBASE III and dBASE III
               Plus.

DBF 4   Used by dBASE IV.

File Page Setup

Purpose

Controls the appearance of the individual document,
including margins, centering, headers, footers, gridlines,
orientation, and size. These settings link to the active
document and save to disk. Use this command before
printing with the File Print command.

To set the appearance of a file

1. Activate the document whose print settings you want
   to adjust.

2. Press Alt, F, T or click the File menu and select Page
   SeTup.

3. Enter a Header or Footer to appear on every page and
   format the headers and footers with codes. (Press F1
   to display the Page Setup Help window, then select
   the headers and footers topic to display a list of
   codes.)

   Change the Left, Right, Top, and Bottom margins (in
   inches). Use decimal fractions if needed. Turn on
   Center Horizontally and Center Vertically to print the
   document centered between the margins.

   Turn on Row & Column Headings to print the Row
   numbers and Column letters on each page.

   Turn on Gridlines to print horizontal and vertical
   lines along the rows and columns on each page.

   Select the POrtrait option to print the document down
   the length of the paper; select the Landscape option
   to print the document across the width of the paper.

   Choose letter, legal, or ledger paper size from the
   Paper drop-down list.

Specify the percentage of reduction or enlargement (if supported by your printer).

Turn on FIt To Page to compress the document to a single page (if supported by your printer).

4. Press **Enter** or click OK.

Excel links your settings with the document and saves them.

Note

See also **Help** commands.

File Print

Purpose

Prints the active document.

To print a file

1. Activate the document you want to print.

2. Prepare worksheets for printing by using the **O**ptions Set Page **B**reak and **O**ptions Set Print **A**rea commands.

   Use the **F**ile P**R**inter Setup and **F**ile Page Se**T**up commands to adjust your printer options.

3. Press **Alt, F, P** or press **Alt-Ctrl-Shift-F2** or press **Ctrl-Shift-F12** or click the **F**ile menu and select **P**rint.

   The current printer setting appears in a dialog box.

   In the Print screen, you can specify the following print options:

   Enter the number of **C**opies you want to print (the default is one copy).

   Choose between printing **A**ll pages or selected pages. If you want to print selected pages, enter the page span in the **F**rom **T**o boxes.

Turn on **D**raft Quality to print with lower resolution
but greater speed (if supported by your printer).

Choose to print the **S**heet values but not the cell
notes, the **N**otes alone, or **B**oth the values and the
notes.

Select **P**review and press **Enter** or click OK to see
how the printed document will look, including where
page breaks will occur, before you print. See File
Print Pre**V**iew command.

4. Print by pressing **Enter** or clicking OK.

═║ File Print Preview ║═══════════

Purpose

Displays each page as it will look when printed.

To preview the printed page

1. Activate the document you want to preview.

2. Press **Alt**, **F**, **V** or click the **F**ile menu and select
   Pre**V**iew.

   Choose from the following options:

   The **N**ext button displays the next page of the
   document.

   Previous displays the preceding page of the
   document.

   Zoom switches between full page view and actual
   size view.

   Prin**T** displays the **F**ile Prin**T** dialog box and prints
   the document.

   Setup displays the **F**ile Page Se**T**up dialog box.

   Margins allows you to adjust margins and column
   widths by dragging the markers.

   Close closes the Print Preview window and displays
   the active document.

File Printer Setup

Purpose

Identifies installed printers and allows you to change certain default printer settings. This command controls default printer settings for all applications and documents. To control printer settings for a single document, use the File Page SeTup command.

To set printer configuration

1. Press Alt, F, R or click the File menu and select PRinter Setup.

2. Select the Printer you want to use.

3. Select Setup for more options. The options available depend on the printer you select.

4. Make appropriate changes and then press Enter or click OK.

   Excel saves the settings and returns to the first dialog box.

5. Press Enter or click OK to return to the document.

File Record Macro

Purpose

When all files are closed, duplicates the Macro ReCord command (records your Excel actions in a macro file). This command makes it easy to create and name a macro, but offers less control over where Excel stores the macro than the Macro Start Recorder command.

To record a macro

1. Plan the macro you want to record.

2. Press Alt, F, C or click the File menu and select ReCord Macro.

3. Accept the suggested macro name (Record followed by a number) or type a different name.

4. Accept the suggested letter assigned to the macro, or type a different letter.

5. When you are ready to begin recording your macro, press **Enter** or click OK.

6. Perform the actions you want to record.

   If a macro sheet was open before you started, the macro records on the sheet starting at the top of the next completely empty column. If no macro sheet was open, Excel opens a new sheet and starts recording in cell A1.

7. After you finish, press **Alt**, **M**, **C** or click the **M**acro menu and select Stop Re**C**order.

8. You can run the macro by pressing **Ctrl-** plus the letter you assigned the macro or by using the **M**acro **R**un command.

9. Save the macro sheet before you exit Excel.

Note

The Record Ma**C**ro command is available under the **F**ile menu only after all documents have been closed. If any documents are open, the Re**C**ord command is found under the **M**acro menu.

File Save

Purpose

Saves a file to disk as you continue to work. If the file has already been named, changes are saved immediately. If the file has not been named, displays a dialog box of saving options.

To save a file

Press **Alt**, **F**, **S** or press **Alt-Shift-F2** or press **Shift-F12** or click the **F**ile menu and select **S**ave.

Caution

>   Save about every 15 minutes so that you lose no more
>   than this much work if your power source fails.

File Save As

Purpose

>   Saves a file to disk. Always displays a dialog box of
>   saving options. Enables you to duplicate an existing
>   document by saving the file with a different file name.

To save a file

1. Press **Alt**, **F**, **A** or press **Alt-F2** or press **F12** or click
    the **F**ile menu and select Save **A**s.

    A dialog box appears.

2. Accept the suggested directory and file name or type
    another directory and file name.

3. Press **Enter** or click OK

    or

    Select **O**ptions and select a file format from the **F**ile
    Format drop-down list. (Press **F1** to display the Save
    As Help window, then select the file format topic to
    display a list of file format options.)

Protect the file by assigning a **P**assword of up to 16
letters, numbers, and symbols. Unless you have the
password, you cannot access the file while it is
password-protected.

Create **B**ackup Files to save the preceding version of
your file on disk by renaming the file with a .BAK
extension.

After you finish, press **Enter** or click OK. The file is
saved according to your settings.

Note

For periodic saving of an existing document under the default options, File Save is faster.

See also Help commands.

File Save Workspace ═══════════

Purpose

Saves the position and size of all open windows in the Excel workspace. All open documents are saved in individual files. You can retrieve all documents as they appeared when you issued the command by opening the workspace file. Workspace files are assigned the extension XLW.

To save a workspace

1. Press **Alt**, **F**, **W** or click the **F**ile menu and select Save **W**orkspace.

   A dialog box appears asking you to supply a file name. If this file is new, Excel suggests the default name RESUME.XLW. If this workspace file already exists, Excel suggests the current name.

2. To accept the suggested name, press **Enter** or click OK. To use a different file name, type the name and then press **Enter** or click OK.

   All open documents are saved individually, and the workspace information is saved in the new file you create. You can exit Excel, then later reestablish your documents and workspace by selecting **F**ile **O**pen and the name of your workspace file.

Caution

A workspace file contains a list of the documents that were open when the workspace file was created, not the documents themselves. If you close a workspace file, Excel will prompt you to save changes made to any of the individual files.

File Unhide

Purpose

When all files are closed, lists hidden files. Makes the file you select visible.

To display a hidden file

1. Press Alt, F, U or click the File menu and select Unhide.

   A list of hidden files appears. The command is dimmed if no files are hidden.

2. Select the file you want to see and press Enter or click OK.

To hide an open window

Select the Window Hide command

Note

If a file is open and another file is hidden, the Unhide command is found under the Window menu. The Unhide command is dimmed if no files are hidden.

Format 3-D View

Purpose

Controls the angle at which you view the data in a three-dimensional chart.

To set the view angle for a 3-D chart

1. Press Alt, T, 3 or click the FormaT menu and select 3-D View. This command is available only if the active chart is a 3-D chart.

2. Make changes using the Elevation, Rotation, Right Angle AXes, and Height choices in the dialog box.

3. Select Apply to change current settings in the active chart without closing the dialog box.

Select Default to retrieve the original chart settings.

4. Press Enter or click OK

    Select Close or press Esc to cancel the 3-D View
    dialog box without making any changes to the chart.

Note

If you change the chart type using the Gallery menu, the
3-D View formats are not reset to their original values.

Format Alignment

Purpose

Sets the alignment of selected cells.

To set cell alignment

1. Select the cells you want to align. (To select the entire
    worksheet, press Ctrl-Shift-space bar.)

2. Select one of the following options:

General	Aligns text left, numbers right, and logical values and errors center.
Left, Center, or Right	Aligns all types of cell contents left, center, or right.
Fill	Repeats the contents of the cell until the display is full. (With a cell width of 9, for example, 123 displays as 123123123, but the value of 123 is unaffected.)

    The default alignment is General.

3. Select the Word Wrap check box if you want text to
    wrap according to the column width, increasing the
    row height.

4. Press Enter or click OK.

Note

Blank cells that are part of a Fill range display the contents of the cells to their left. You can use this feature to create a border with a character or a mix of characters.

Format Border

Purpose

Adds lines, boxes, and shading to selected cells.

To format borders

1. Select the cells you want to format with a border. (To select the entire worksheet, press **Ctrl-Shift-space bar**.)

2. Press **Alt**, **T**, **B** or click the Forma**T** menu and select **B**order.

3. Select one or more of the following options:

Outline	Draws a rectangular box around the range of cells.
Left	Draws a line to the left of each cell.
Right	Draws a line to the right of each cell.
Top	Draws a line above each cell.
Bottom	Draws a line below each cell.

4. Select Styl**E** and **C**olor options. Check the **S**hade box if you want the border to be shaded.

5. Press **Enter** or click OK.

Format Bring To Front

Purpose

Places selected object in front of all other objects.

To bring an object to the front

1. Select the object in the background that you want to bring to the foreground. (This command has no effect if the selected object is already in front.)

2. Press **Alt**, **T**, **F** or click the FormaT menu and select Bring To FrOnt.

Format Cell Protection

Purpose

Protects selected cells and their formulas. This command is available only when cells are selected and the Options Protect Document command has not been executed.

To protect selected cells

1. Select the cells you want to protect. (To select the entire worksheet, press **Ctrl-Shift-space bar**.)

2. Press **Alt**, **T**, **P** or click the FormaT menu and select Cell Protection.

3. Turn on the Locked option to prevent editing of the cell contents. The default is Locked cells.

4. Turn on the Hidden option to prevent the formulas in the cells from appearing in the formula bar and Info window.

5. Press **Enter** or click OK.

6. Select the Options Protect Document command and turn on Cells.

Format Column Width

Purpose

Sets the display width of selected columns (does not affect how much data the columns can hold).

To set column width

1. Select at least one cell from each of the columns you want to change. (To change the width of all columns in the worksheet, select one entire row by pressing **Shift-space bar**.)

2. Press **Alt**, **T**, **C** or click the FormaT menu and select Column Width.

3. To specify a new column width, type a number from 0 to 255 indicating the number of characters you want to appear in a cell. Your number can include decimal fractions, which represent fractions of a character.

   If a column is too narrow to display the contents, the column will display multiple pound signs (####). You can view the data in the formula bar and the Info window.

4. Turn on the Standard Width option to reset the columns (to 8.43 characters).

5. Select Hide to set the column width to zero and remove the column from view.

   If a column is hidden, select the column headings on both sides of the hidden column and select the Unhide command to display the hidden column.

6. Select Best Fit if you want the column width to adjust to the widest cell in the column.

   With the mouse, double-click the right border of the column heading to adjust the column width for the Best Fit.

7. Press **Enter** or click OK.

To set column width with the mouse

With the mouse, change a column's width by clicking and dragging the right border of the column heading.

Format Font ═══════════════════

Purpose

Changes the font for selected cells, chart text, or the entire document.

To change the font

1. Select the cells or chart text whose fonts you want to change.

2. Press **Alt**, **T**, **F** or click the Forma**T** menu and select **F**ont.

3. Select the **F**ont, Si**Z**e, **C**olor, and Style choices from the dialog box. A document can use up to 256 fonts.

   Turn on P**R**inter Fonts to display only the fonts that your printer can print. If you select fonts that your printer cannot print, the printer will use the closest font type to the one that you selected.

   A sample of your choices appears in the sample area.

4. Press **Enter** or click OK.

Format Group ═══════════════════

Purpose

Creates a single graphic object from several selected graphic objects. This command is available only when the active document is a worksheet or a macro sheet.

To group objects

1. Select the objects you want to group. Use the selection tool on the tool bar or hold down the **Shift** key as you select objects.

   The command is dimmed when only one object is selected.

2. Press **Alt**, **T**, **G** or click the Forma**T** menu and select Group. (Forma**T** Ungroup appears when a grouped object is selected.)

   The selected objects are now grouped as a single object and can be moved, sized, and formatted as one object.

Format Justify

Purpose

Changes column text into a word-wrapped paragraph.

To justify column text

1. Select a range of cells containing text as the leftmost column and blank cells in the rest of the range.

2. Press **Alt**, **T**, **J** or click the Forma**T** menu and select Justify.

   The text in the range's lower rows moves and combines with the text in the upper rows to the extent permitted by the width of the range.

   Blank cells in the text column act as separators, creating multiple paragraphs. (The cells must be blank, rather than containing spaces.)

Format Legend

Purpose

Changes the position of the active chart's legend.

To move the legend with the keyboard

1. Select the legend.

2. Press **Alt, T, L** or click the FormaT menu and select **L**egend.

3. Select the position of the legend: at the chart's **B**ottom, (top right) **C**orner, or **T**op, or **R**ight (standing vertical) or **L**eft. The default position is **R**ight.

4. To accept your settings and return to the chart, press **Enter** or click OK.

    To accept your settings and move on to another chart FormaT command, select the **P**atterns or **FO**nt button.

To move the legend with the mouse

With the mouse, click and drag the legend to any position on the chart.

Format Main Chart

Purpose

Sets the active main chart's type and formatting and enables you to change chart types without losing custom formatting.

To format a main chart

1. Press **Alt, T, M** or click the FormaT menu and select **M**ain Chart.

2. Select one of 10 Chart Types: Area, Bar, Column, Line, Pie, XY (Scatter), 3-D Area, 3-D Column, 3-D Line, or 3-D Pie.

3. The options vary depending on the chart type.

    Choose from the available options:

Data VIew	Shows available marker arrangements for the selected chart type.
Overlap	Determines overlap of markers in a bar or column chart.
Gap Width	Determines space between clusters in a bar or column chart.
Vary by Categories	Gives each data point in a single series a different color.
Drop Lines	Extends lines from the highest value in each category to the category axis.
Hi-Lo Lines	Extends lines from the highest to the lowest value in each category.
AnglE of First Pie Slice (degrees)	Sets the angle of the first edge of the first slice in a pie chart.
3-D Gap Depth	Sets distance between data series is a 3-D chart.
3-D Chart Depth	Set depth of a 3-D chart relative to its width.

    The default is a Column chart with all other options turned off and % Cluster SpacIng set at 50 percent.

4. Press Enter or click OK.

Format Move

Purpose

Enables you to move the active chart's objects.

To move a chart object

1. Select the chart object you want to move.

2. Press **Alt, T, M** or click the Forma**T** menu and select Move.

3. Press the arrow keys to reposition the object. Press **Ctrl-** plus the arrow keys to move in smaller increments.

   With the mouse, click and drag the object.

4. When the object is in the desired location, press **Enter**.

Format Number

Purpose

Sets the number, date, or time format of the values in selected cells.

To format numbers

1. Select the cells whose numeric, date, or time values you want to format. (To select the entire worksheet, press **Ctrl-Shift-space bar**.)

2. Press **Alt, T, N** or click the Forma**T** menu and select Number.

   The Format Number box offers you a list of 23 different formats, including integers, scientific notation, currency, percentages, dates, and times. The default format is General.

3. Select one of the formats and press **Enter** or click OK.

Format Object Placement

Purpose

Controls how graphic objects are attached to cells.

To move a graphic object

1. Select the object you want to move.

2. Press **Alt, T, L** or click the Forma**T** menu and select Object P**L**acement.

3. Select the button that describes how you want the object to move and size with the underlying cells.

Format Object Protection

Purpose

Protects the selected object in a worksheet or macro sheet from being moved or modified. This command is available only when an object is selected and the Options Protect Document command has not been executed.

To protect an object

1. Select the object that you want to protect.

2. Press **Alt, T, I** or click the Forma**T** menu and select Object Protect**I**on.

   To prevent the selected object from being protected when the document is protected, turn off the Locked check box.

3. Press **Enter** or click OK.

4. Select the Options Protect Document command and turn on Objects.

Format Overlay

Purpose

Sets the active overlay chart's type and formatting.

To format an overlay chart

1. Activate a chart with an overlay.

2. Press **Alt**, **T**, **O** or click the Forma**T** menu and select **O**verlay.

3. Select from the options in the Format Overlay Chart dialog box.

4. Press **Enter** or click OK.

Format Patterns

Purpose

Sets the style, weight, color, and pattern of the selected object.

To apply formats to an object in a worksheet or macro sheet

1. Select the worksheet object you want to format.

2. Press **Alt**, **T**, **P** or click the Forma**T** menu and select **P**atterns.

   The options vary depending on the selected objects.

3. Choose from the available options:

   Automatic

   None

   Style

   Weight

   Co**L**or

   Pattern

   Foreground

Background

SHadow

Rounded Corners

Arrow Head

4. To accept your settings and return to the worksheet, press **Enter** or click OK.

To apply formats to an item in a chart

1. Select the chart item you want to format.

2. Press **Alt**, **T**, **P** or click the Forma**T** menu and select **P**atterns or double-click the item you want to format.

   The options vary depending on the selected item.

3. Choose from the available options:

   Automatic

   None

   Color

   Style

   Weight

   Pattern

   Foreground

   Background

   InVert if Negative

   Apply To All

   SHadow

   Tick Mark Type

   Tick Labels

   Arrow Head

4. To accept your settings and return to the chart, press **Enter** or click OK.

Format Row Height

Purpose

Sets the height of selected rows.

To set row height with the keyboard

1. Select at least one cell from each row whose height you want to change. (To change the height of all rows in the worksheet, select an entire column by pressing **Ctrl-space bar**.)

2. Press **Alt**, **T**, **R** or click the Forma**T** menu and select **R**ow Height.

3. To specify a new row height, type the height's point size (72 points = 1 inch), which can range from 0 (which hides the rows from view) to 409. Your number can include decimal fractions, which represent fractions of a point.

   Turn on **S**tandard Height to reset the rows (to 12.75 points).

   Select **H**ide to set the row height to zero and remove the row from view. If a row is hidden, select the row headings on both sides of the hidden row and select the **U**nhide command to display the hidden row.

4. Press **Enter** or click OK.

To set row height with the mouse

Change a row's height by clicking and dragging the bottom border of the row's heading.

Format Scale

Purpose

Controls the scale setting for each axis on the active chart.

To set the scale of an axis

1. Select either the category (X) axis, value (Y) axis, or data series axis.

2. Press **Alt, T, S** or click the Forma**T** menu and select **S**cale.

   Different options are available depending on the chart type and axis you are formatting.

3. Select from the following available options:

Category (X)Axis Scale Options

Value Axis **C**rosses at Category Number, which specifies the number of the category where the Value (Y) axis crosses the Category (X) axis (usually 1).

Number of Categories Between Tick **L**abels.

Number of Categories Between Tick Mar**K**s.

Value Axis Crosses **B**etween Categories.

Categories in **R**everse Order, which displays categories from right to left.

Value Axis Crosses at **M**aximum Category, which makes the Value (Y) axis cross the Category (X) axis at the last category.

The **P**atterns, F**O**nt and **T**ext buttons allow you to apply formatting to those elements.

Value (Y) Axis Scale Options

Mi**N**imum and Ma**X**imum values the chart will display.

MA**j**or Unit and M**I**nor Unit for the distance between major and minor tick marks.

Category Axis **C**rosses At for the value where the Category (X) axis crosses the Value (Y) axis.

Whether **L**ogarithmic Scale is used to calculate the preceding settings.

Reverse Order, which displays values in descending order.

Category Axis Crosses at Maximum Value, which makes the Category (X) axis cross the Value (Y) axis at the highest value.

The Patterns, FOnt and Text buttons allow you to apply formatting to those elements.

Data Series Axis Scale Options

(The Data Series axis is the Y axis on a 3-D chart.)

Number of Series Between Tick Labels.

Number of Series Between Tick MarKs.

Series in Reverse Order, which reverses order of the series.

The Patterns, FOnt and Text buttons allow you to apply formatting to those elements.

4. To accept your settings and return to the chart, press Enter or click OK.

Format Send To Back

Purpose

Places selected object behind all other objects.

To place an object in the back

1. Select the object in the foreground that you want to place in the background. (This command has no effect if the selected object is already in the background.)

2. Press Alt, T, E or click the FormaT menu and select SEnd to Back.

The object sent to the back is no longer visible if it is completely covered by another object.

Format Size

Purpose

Enables you to resize chart arrows and unattached text boxes in a chart.

To resize a chart object with the keyboard

1. Select the chart object you want to resize.

2. Press Alt, T, Z or click the FormaT menu and select SiZe.

3. Press the arrow keys to resize the object in either or both dimensions. Press Ctrl- plus the arrow keys to resize in smaller increments.

4. When the object is the correct size, press Enter.

To resize a chart object with the mouse

With the mouse, resize a chart object by clicking and dragging its black selection squares.

Format Style

Purpose

Defines a cell style based on the selected formats and assigns the style a name. (A style can be created in three ways.)

To create a style by example

1. Select a cell that has the desired combination of formats.

2. Press Alt, T, S or click the FormaT menu and select Style.

3. Type a name for the style in the Style Name text box.

4. Press Enter or click OK.

To create a style by example using the tool bar

1. Select a cell that has the desired combination of formats.

2. Select the style name in the Style box at the left end of the tool bar and type a new name for the style. (The default style name is Normal.)

3. Press **Enter**.

To create a style by definition

1. Press **Alt**, **T**, **S** or click the Forma**T** menu and select **Style**.

2. Type a name for the style in the Style dialog box.

3. Select **D**efine. The Style dialog box expands to display six cell attributes.

4. Turn on the check boxes for the cell attributes you want to include in the style.

   If you turn off the check box for an attribute, the corresponding button for that attribute becomes unavailable.

5. Select the button for the attribute you want to add or change.

6. Select the formats you want to use for the selected attribute.

7. Press **Enter** or click OK to confirm your choices for the selected attribute and return to the Style dialog box.

8. Press **Enter** or click OK to define the style and close the dialog box.

Format Text

Purpose

Sets the alignment and orientation of text in a chart or in a text box in a worksheet.

To format text

1. Select the text in a chart or text box in a worksheet that you want to format.

2. Press **Alt**, **T**, **T** or click the Forma**T** menu and select **T**ext.

3. Select horizontal or vertical alignment options. Select Orie**N**tation choice.

   In a chart, you also can specify these options:

   Turn on **A**utomatic Text

   Turn on A**U**tomatic Size

   SHow Key to

4. Press **Enter** or click OK to accept your settings.

Formula Apply Names

Purpose

Replaces formula cell references with designated names.

To apply names

1. Select a cell or range whose formula cell references you want to replace with created or defined names.

2. Press **Alt**, **R**, **A** or click the FoRmula menu and select **A**pply Names.

3. Select the name you want to apply.

4. Choose

   Ignore Relative/Absolute to replace references regardless of their types or **U**se Row and Column Names to apply names to references that are not exact matches.

5. Press **Enter** or click OK.

Formula Create Names

Purpose

Names cells within a range using the text at specified edges of the range.

To create names

1. Enter the names you want to create in the specified location.

2. Select the range.

3. Press **Alt**, **R**, **C** or press **Ctrl-Shift-F3** or click the FoRmula menu and select **C**reate Names.

4. Indicate the location of the names you want to create.

5. Press **Enter** or click OK.

Formula Define Name

Purpose

Names a cell range, value, or formula.

To name a range, value, or formula

1. Select the range, value, or formula you want to name.

2. Press **Alt, R, D** or press **Ctrl-F3** or click the
   Fo**R**mula menu and select **D**efine Name.

3. If you selected a range, name the selected range.

4. After defining names, press **Enter** or click OK.

Note

This command also enables you to edit and delete
existing names.

Formula Find

Purpose

Finds the next occurrence of the specified text.

To find a specified text or number

1. Select the range whose contents you want to search.

2. Press **Alt, R, F** or press **Shift-F5** or click the
   Fo**R**mula menu and select **F**ind.

3. Type the text or number you want to find in the Find
   What box. You can include the DOS wildcards.

4. Select whether to search in **F**ormulas, **V**alues,
   or **N**otes.

5. Select **WH**ole or **P**art.

6. Select whether to search by **RO**ws or **C**olumns.

7. Press **Enter** or click OK.

8. To find the next occurrence, press **F7**. To find the preceding occurrence, press **Shift-F7**.

9. Repeat Step 8 to find all occurrences.

Formula Goal Seek

Purpose

Varies the value in a specified cell until a formula dependent on that cell reaches the desired value.

To solve for a desired result

1. Select the cell containing the formula for which you want to find a specific solution.

2. Press **Alt**, **R**, **L** or click the FoRmula menu and select GoaL Seek.

3. Enter the value you want the formula to produce in the To Value box.

4. Enter the cell reference or select the cell containing the value (not a formula) that you want Excel to change to produce the specified result.

5. Press **Enter** or click OK.

6. Press **Enter** or click OK. Press **Esc** or click Cancel to keep the old value.

Formula Goto

Purpose

Locates and selects the specified named range.

To go to a named range

1. Press **Alt**, **R**, **G** or press **F5** or click the FoRmula menu and select Goto.

2. Select a name from the list or type a name or a cell address in the **R**eference box.

3. Press **Enter** or click OK.

Formula Note

Purpose

Enables you to add, view, edit, and delete notes in a cell.

To add or edit a note

1. Select the cell in which you want to add or edit a note.

2. Press **Alt**, **R**, **N** or press **Shift-F2** or click the Fo**R**mula menu and select **N**ote.

3. Add text or edit the existing text in the **N**ote dialog box.

4. Press **Enter** or click OK to accept the changes and close the dialog box. Press **A**dd to accept the changes and keep the dialog box open.

Caution

Selecting Cancel closes the dialog box, but does not undo editing, additions, or deletions you made.

Formula Outline

Purpose

Creates an outline from an existing worksheet or range.

To create an outline

1. Select the range you want to outline. If you select a single cell, Excel outlines the entire worksheet.

2. Press **Alt**, **R**, **O** or click the Fo**R**mula menu and select **O**utline.

3. Turn on the Automatic Styles check box if you want Excel to apply built-in outline styles. Specify the direction you want the levels to flow in the outline.

4. Select Create.

Formula Paste Function

Purpose

Lists all predefined Excel worksheet formulas and inserts the selected formula and (optionally) its arguments in the formula bar.

To paste a function into a cell

1. Select the cell in which you want to paste the formula.

2. Press Alt, R, T or press Shift-F3 or click the FoRmula menu and select PasTe Function.

3. Select the name of the function you want to insert (jump to a function by pressing its first letter).

4. To insert only the function name in the formula bar, press Enter or click OK. To include the arguments, turn on Paste Arguments and press Enter or click OK.

5. If you included the argument names, replace the argument placeholders with the appropriate arguments.

Formula Paste Name

Purpose

Lists all worksheet names and inserts the selected name in the formula bar.

To paste a name into a cell

1. Select the cell in which you want to build a formula using a defined name.

2. Press **Alt**, **R**, **P** or press **F3** or click the Fo**R**mula menu and select **P**aste Name.

3. Select the name you want (jump to a name by pressing its first letter).

4. To insert the selected name in the formula bar, press **Enter** or click OK. The name appears in the formula bar. Complete the formula and press **Enter**.

5. To insert a list of all defined names and their references in the worksheet starting at the active cell, select Paste **L**ist.

Formula Reference

Purpose

Changes selected references in the formula bar.

To change the type of a reference

1. Select the cell containing the reference you want to edit. Press **F2** and select the cell reference you want to change.

2. Press **Alt**, **R**, **R** or press **F4** or click the Fo**R**mula menu and select **R**eference.

3. Repeat Step 2 until you obtain the desired cell reference.

Formula Replace

Purpose

Searches for the specified text or number and replaces it with another text or number.

To replace a specified text or number

1. Select the range whose contents you want to search and replace.

2. Press **Alt**, **R**, **E** or click the Fo**R**mula menu and select R**E**place.

3. Type the text or number you want to replace in the Find **W**hat box. You can include DOS wildcards.

4. Type the replacement text or number in the Re**P**lace With dialog box.

5. Select **WH**ole or **P**art.

6. Select whether to search by R**O**ws or **C**olumns.

7. To find the next occurrence, select **F**ind Next. To find the preceding occurrence, press and hold **Shift** and select **F**ind Next.

8. To replace the current occurrence and then find the next occurrence, select **R**eplace. Continue this procedure to replace all further occurrences.

   When Excel finds no more matches, press **Enter** or click OK to clear the dialog box.

9. Select Replace **A**ll to replace all occurrences of the text. If you do not like the results, select **E**dit **U**ndo Replace.

10. After making replacements, press **Esc** or click Close to close the Re**P**lace With dialog box.

Formula Select Special

Purpose

Selects all cells that fit the specified description.

To select cells

1. Select the range you want to search. If you do not select a range, Excel searches the entire worksheet.

2. Press **Alt**, **R**, **S** or click the Fo**R**mula menu and select the **S**elect Special command.

3. Choose whether to select cells containing **N**otes, **C**onstants, Fo**R**mulas (formula **NU**mbers, **T**ext, **L**ogicals or **E**rrors), or **B**lanks.

Or select Current RegiOn, Current Array, RoW Differences, or ColuMn Differences.

Or select Precedents or Dependents at the DIrect Only level or at All LeVels.

Or select LaSt Cell, Visible Cells, or OBjects.

4. Press Enter or click OK.

Formula Show Active Cell

Purpose

Scrolls the worksheet until the active cell is in view.

To display the active cell

Press Alt, R, H or click the FoRmula menu and select SHow Active Cell.

Formula Solver

Purpose

Solves for a specific solution.

To solve for a specified solution

1. Select the cell whose value you want to maximize, minimize, or reach a certain value.

2. Press Alt, R, V or click the FoRmula menu and select SolVer.

3. Select the Maximize, MiNimize, or Value option. If the Value option is selected, enter the desired value in the box.

4. Select the cell(s) that can be adjusted by Solver.

5. Select cell(s) that are subject to constraints and specify the constraints. The Options button controls advanced features of the solution process.

6. Select Solve to initiate the problem solving process
    for the defined problem. Reset clears all settings from
    the dialog box. OK closes the dialog box without
    activating Solver and saves the settings. Cancel closes
    the dialog box without saving the settings.

Gallery

Purpose

Lists chart types and enables selection among several
predefined formats for each chart type.

To select a predefined chart format

1. Press Alt, G or click the Gallery menu and select the
    chart type you want to use.

    Excel displays several predefined formats for that
    chart type. To see the formats for other chart types on
    the Gallery menu, select Next or Previous.

2. Double-click the chart format you want to use or
    select the chart and press Enter or click OK.

    Excel applies the format to the active chart. If the
    active chart has an overlay, the overlay is deleted.

Gallery Preferred

Purpose

Applies the format you defined with the Gallery SeT
Preferred command to the active chart.

To apply the preferred chart format

Press Alt, G, R or click the Gallery menu and
select Preferred.

Gallery Set Preferred

Purpose

Changes the default chart format to one that you specify.

To set the preferred chart format

1. Create a chart that uses the chart type and formats that you want to use as the default for all new charts.

2. Press **Alt, G, T** or click the **G**allery menu and select SeT Preferred. Select the **G**allery P**R**eferred command to apply your selected format to the active chart.

Caution

The preferred format is lost when you exit Excel, unless you use the **F**ile Save **W**orkspace command to save the workspace.

Help

Purpose

Displays a help for Excel topics.

To locate and display Excel help topics

1. Press **Alt, H, I** or click the **H**elp menu and select Index.

2. To close the Help window, press **Alt, F, X** or press **Alt-F4** or click the **F**ile menu and select E**X**it.

To display Excel equivalents of Lotus 1-2-3 commands

1. Press **Alt, H, L** or click the **H**elp menu and select Lotus 123.

2. Choose the Instruction or Demonstration option. Select Faster or Slower buttons (1-5) to control the

speed of the demonstration. Choose the More **H**elp
button for a list of topics for assistance.

3. Select the Lotus 1-2-3 command you want to
    perform.

To run the help tutorial

1. Press **Alt**, **H**, **T** or click the **H**elp menu and
    select **T**utorial.

2. Press **Enter** or click OK to save any open
    document(s).

3. Select the topic for which you want help.

4. To quit the Help Tutorial, press **X** or click the Exit
    Tutorial button (from the Main Menu) or press **Ctrl-
    F1**, **X** or click the Controls button and then the Exit
    Tutorial button (from a lesson).

═| Info |══════════════════

Purpose

Displays information about the active cell.

To display information about the active cell

1. Select the cell whose information you want to
    display.

2. Press **Alt**, **W**, **S** or click the **W**indow menu and select
    Show Info.

3. Select one of the Info commands.

4. Press **Ctrl-F4** or click the Info window Control menu
    bar and select **C**lose to close the Info window and
    return to the menu bar.

Macro Absolute (Relative) Record

Purpose

Absolute Record records macro cell references as
absolute references. This command appears only when
you select Macro RelAtive Record while operating in
Full Menus.

Relative Record records macro cell references as relative
references. This command appears only when you select
Macro Absolute Record while operating in Full Menus.

You can select these commands before and during
macro recording.

To record absolute references

Press Alt, M, A or click the Macro menu and select
Absolute Record.

To record relative references

Press Alt, M, A or click the Macro menu and select
RelAtive Record. This command is the default setting.

Macro Assign to Object

Purpose

Assigns a macro to an object.

To assign a macro to an object

1. Open the macro sheet containing the macro that you
   want to assign to the object.

2. Select the graphic object in which you want to attach
   the macro.

3. Press Alt, M, O or click to Macro menu and select
   Assign to Object.

4. Select the macro from the Assign Macro box or type the macro name in the ReFerence box.

5. Press Enter or click OK.

Macro Record

Purpose

Records your Excel commands and keystrokes on a macro sheet.

To record a macro

1. Plan the macro you want to record.

2. Press Alt, M, C or click the Macro menu and select ReCord.

3. Type a Name for the macro or accept the default.

4. Type a shortcut Key for the macro or accept the default.

5. When you are ready to perform the actions, press Enter or click OK.

6. Perform the actions you want to record.

7. After performing the actions, press Alt, M, C again or click the Macro menu and select Stop ReCorder.

   To view the macro sheet after the macro is recorded, press Alt, W and select the macro sheet.

8. To run the macro, press Ctrl plus the shortcut key or select the Macro Run command and then select the macro name.

9. To save the macro, save its macro sheet with the File Save command.

Macro Run

Purpose

Lists all named macros on open macro sheets and runs the macro you select.

To run a macro

1. Press **Alt**, **M**, **R** or click the **M**acro menu and select **R**un.

2. Select the macro you want to run from the **R**un list or type the complete macro name.

   Select **S**tep if you want the macro to execute one step at a time.

3. Press **Enter** or click OK.

Macro Set Recorder

Purpose

Defines a range in a macro sheet for storing macros recorded with the **M**acro **S**tart Recorder command.

To set a range on a macro sheet

1. Activate the macro sheet that will store the macro.

2. Select the range in the macro sheet in which you want to record.

3. Press **Alt**, **M**, **T** or click the **M**acro menu and select Se**T** Recorder.

Macro Start Recorder

Purpose

Records your Excel actions on a macro sheet.

To record a macro

1. Plan the macro you want to record.

2. Activate a new or existing macro sheet.

3. Select the range in the macro sheet in which you want to record the macro and select Macro SeT Recorder.

4. Activate the document in which you want to perform your actions.

5. Press Alt, M, S or click the Macro menu and select Start Recorder.

6. Perform the actions you want to record.

7. Press Alt, M, C or click the Macro menu and select Stop ReCorder.

8. To run the macro select the Macro Run command.

9. To save the macro, use the File Save command.

Options Calculate Document

Purpose

Forces calculation in the active document.

To recalculate the active document

Press Alt, Shift-O, N or press Shift-F9 or press Shift, click the Options menu, and select Calculate DocumeNt.

Options Calculate Now

Purpose

Forces calculation in all open worksheets and charts or in selected formulas.

To recalculate worksheets and charts

Press Alt, O, N or press F9 or click the Options menu and select Calculate Now.

Options Calculation

Purpose

Controls how Excel calculates formulas.

To set calculation options

1. Press Alt, O, C or click the Options menu and select Calculation.

2. Select Automatic, Automatic except Tables, or Manual.

3. Select iteration limits. Excel's defaults are 100 for Maximum ItErations and 0.001 for Maximum Charge.

4. Turn on or off the following features:

   Update Remote References
   Precision as Displayed
   1904 Date System
   Save External Link Values

5. Press Enter or click OK.

Options Color Palette

Purpose

Customizes colors and copies color palettes.

To change a color

1. Press Alt, O, E or click the Options menu and select Color PalEtte.

2. Select a color in the palette and choose the Edit command.

3. Select another color from the color box. Increase or decrease Hue, Saturation, Luminosity, and Red, Green, and Blue color tones.

4. When the sample rectangle displays the color you want, press Enter or click OK.

To copy a color palette

1. Press **Alt-C** or click the **C**opy Colors From arrow to see all open documents.

2. Select the document from which you want to copy the color palette. Press **Enter** or click OK.

To reset the color palette

The **D**efault button in the Color Pal**E**tte dialog box resets the color palette to its original 16 colors.

Options Display

Purpose

Controls display of cells and objects and enables you to turn on or off gridlines and column and row headings.

To set display options

1. Press **Alt**, **O**, **D** or click the **O**ptions menu and select **D**isplay.

2. Turn on the display options you want to use.

3. Press **Enter** or click OK.

Options Freeze (Unfreeze) Panes

Purpose

Freeze panes stops the scrolling of the top and left panes of a divided worksheet created with the Control **S**plit command. This command keeps row or column titles stationary. Unfreeze panes reverses the action of the **O**ptions **F**reeze Panes command, enabling scrolling in all window panes.

To freeze or unfreeze panes

Press **Alt**, **O**, **F** or click the **O**ptions menu and select **F**reeze (or Un**F**reeze) Panes.

Note

See also Control SpliT.

Options Full (Short) Menus

Purpose

Full menus sets all menus to display all options. Short Menus sets all menus to display the most-used options only.

To set the menu display

Press Alt, O, M or click the Options menu and select Full (Short) Menus.

Options Protect (Unprotect) Document

Purpose

Sets (or removes) protection for a document's cells. Sets (or removes) password protection.

To protect a document

1. Press Alt, O, P or click the Options menu and select Protect Document.

2. Select Cells to protect or unprotect the cell as specified by the FormaT Cell Protection dialog box.

3. Select Windows to protect or unprotect the document window screen position, size, and other characteristics.

4. Select Objects to protect or unprotect objects specified with the FormaT Object ProtectIon command.

5. To protect your protection settings, select Password and enter any combination of letters, spaces, numbers, or symbols.

You cannot change or unprotect the document unless you use the password. Passwords are case-sensitive.

6. Press Enter or click OK.

To unprotect a document

1. Press Alt, O, P or click the Options menu and select UnProtect Document.

2. If the document is not password-protected, you can now alter the document.

   If Excel requests a password, type the appropriate password and press Enter or click OK.

Options Set (Remove) Page Break

Purpose

Inserts (or deletes) a manual page break.

To set a page break

1. Select the cell to the right and below where you want to insert a page break.

2. Press Alt, O, B or click the Options menu and select Set Page Break.

To remove a page break

1. Position the cell pointer directly below or to the right of the page break you want to remove. (The Options Remove Page Break command appears only when the cell pointer is in this position.)

2. Press Alt, O, B or click the Options menu and select Remove Page Break.

   This command works on manual page breaks only. You cannot remove automatic page breaks.

Options Set (Remove) Print Area

Purpose

Set Print Area specifies the area of the worksheet to be printed. Remove Print Area deletes the specification of the print area.

To set the print area

1. Select the worksheet area you want to print.

2. Press **Alt**, **O**, **A** or click the **O**ptions menu and select Set Print **A**rea.

    Dashed lines outline the print area, and Excel internally names the section Print_Area.

3. Repeat Steps 1 and 2 to define a new print area.

To remove the print area

1. Press **Ctrl-Shift-space bar** or click in the upper left corner of the worksheet in the cell where the row and column headings intersect to select the worksheet.

2. Press **Alt**, **O**, **A** or click the **O**ptions menu and select Remove Print **A**rea. **O**ptions Remove Print **A**rea appears only when the entire worksheet is selected.

Options Set (Remove) Print Titles

Purpose

Specifies (or deletes) title text to be printed on every page of a worksheet.

To set print titles

1. Enter the title text in the worksheet you want to print.
   If the text is in adjoining rows or columns, you can
   include text from anywhere in the worksheet.

2. Select the entire row(s) or column(s) containing the
   title text.

   With the mouse, select entire rows or columns by
   clicking and dragging their headings.

3. Press **Alt, O, T** or click the **O**ptions menu and select
   Set Print **T**itles.

   Excel internally names the section Print_Titles. Text
   in a title cell prints near the top or to the left of every
   page that contains a worksheet cell in the same
   column or row.

To remove print titles

1. Press **Ctrl-Shift-space bar** or click in the upper left
   corner of the worksheet in the cell where the row and
   column headings intersect to select the worksheet.

2. Press **Alt, O, T** or click the **O**ptions menu and select
   Remove Print **T**itles. **O**ptions Remove Print **T**itles
   appears only when the entire worksheet is selected.

Caution

Do not include the titles when you set the print area
because the titles wll print twice.

Options Workspace

Purpose

Determines decimal and workspace settings that apply to
all documents and the surrounding workspace.

To set the number of decimal places

1. Press **Alt, O, W** or click the **O**ptions menu and
   select **W**orkspace.

2. Select Fixed Decimal and enter the number of decimal places you want in the Places text box. The default for Fixed Decimal is off. The default for Places is 2 decimal places. This command does not affect numbers in which you manually insert a decimal point.

3. Select R1C1 to display headings and cell references in Row-Column format rather than in Excel's default A1 format. The default setting is off.

4. Select Status Bar to turn on the status display at the bottom of the screen. The default setting is on.

5. Select Tool Bar to display the tool bar. The default setting is on.

6. Select SCroll Bars to turn on the scroll bar display. The default setting is on.

7. Select FoRmula Bar to turn on the display/editing area at the top of documents. The default setting is on.

8. Select Note InDicator to display a small dot in the top right corner of cells with notes attached. The default setting is on.

9. Change the Alternate Menu key, which duplicates the Alt key's action of selecting the menu bar. Select whether Microsoft EXcel Menus or Lotus 1-2-3 Help displays when you press the slash (/) key. The default setting is Microsoft EXcel Menus.

10. Select Alternate Navigation Keys to provide a different set of keystrokes for spreadsheet navigation. The default setting is off.

11. Select Ignore Remote Requests to ignore or respond to other Windows applications. The default setting is off.

12. Select Move Selection after Enter to move the active cell down one row after data is entered in a cell. The default setting is on.

13. Press Enter or click OK.

Window Activate Window

Purpose

Lists open documents and enables you to activate
a window.

To activate a window

1. Press **Alt**, **W** or click the **W**indow menu to display up
   to nine open windows.

2. Activate a particular window by typing the number to
   its left, by clicking the document name, or by
   pressing **Ctrl-F6** .

Window Arrange All

Purpose

Rearranges all on-screen windows to take maximum
advantage of available space.

To rearrange windows

Press **Alt**, **W**, **A** or click the **W**indow menu and select
Arrange All.

Window Hide (Unhide)

Purpose

Hide makes the active window invisible. The document
remains open and can be unhidden. Unhide lists all
hidden windows and displays the window that you
select.

To hide the active window

Press **Alt**, **W**, **H** or click the **W**indow menu and
select **H**ide.

To unhide a window

1. Press **Alt**, **W**, **U** or click the **W**indow menu and select **U**nhide. (If all windows are hidden, this command appears on the **F**ile menu.)

2. Select the window you want to display and press **Enter** or click OK.

   For windows protected with the **O**ptions **P**rotect Document command and a password, Excel asks for the password before unhiding the window.

Window More Windows

Purpose

Lists the names of all windows, and activates the window you select. This command appears only when more than nine windows are open.

To list window names

1. Press **Alt**, **W**, **M** or click the **W**indow menu and select **M**ore Windows.

2. Select the window you want to activate.

3. Press **Enter** or click OK.

Window New Window

Purpose

Creates an additional window for the active document.

To create a window

1. Press **Alt**, **W**, **N** or click the **W**indow menu and select **N**ew Window.

2. To create additional windows, repeat this procedure.

3. To activate a window, click a visible window or
    select a window from the Window menu or press
    Ctrl-F6 repeatedly.

4. For synchronized scrolling, select Control SpliT.

═ **Window Show (Info) Document**

Purpose

Window Show Info displays the Info window, which
displays information about the active worksheet or
macro sheets.

Window Show Document activates the worksheet
referenced by the Info window, but does not close the
Info window. This command appears only when the Info
window is the active window.

To show the info window

1. Press **Alt, W, S** or press **Ctrl-F2** or click the Window
    menu and select Show Info or click the document.

2. Read the information about the active cell's
    reference, formula, and notes.

3. Select the Info menu by pressing **Alt, I** or click on
    Info and select the appropriate commands to see
    more information.

To activate the worksheet or macro sheet

Press **Alt, W, S** or click the Window menu and select
Show Document.

═ **Window Workgroup**

Purpose

Groups designated worksheets and macro sheets,
enabling changes in the active sheet to be duplicated
throughout the workgroup.

To group worksheets and macro sheets

1. Open all sheets to be included in the workgroup.

2. Activate the sheet in which you want to make changes.

3. Press **Alt**, **W**, **W** or click **W**indow and select **W**orkgroup.

4. Select the sheets you want to include in the workgroup. A workgroup must contain two or more sheets.

5. Press **Enter** or click OK.

To use workgroup mode

The **W**indow **A**rrange All command changes to **W**indow **A**rrange Workgroup and displays only those documents in the workgroup.

The **E**dit Fill Work**G**roup command copies the selection on the active sheet to the same area on all workgroup sheets.

Drawing operations are not available.

You can save a workgroup as a workspace using the **F**ile Save **W**orkspace command. If you activate another document, you exit workgroup mode.

WORKSHEET FUNCTIONS

This section alphabetically lists and briefly describes all Excel worksheet functions. These functions are predefined formulas that can be included in your worksheet formulas.

Functions receive and send data through variables called *arguments*. Each function has a list of arguments, which are enclosed in parentheses and follow the function name. In this book, the names of mandatory arguments appear in bold italic print. The names of optional arguments appear in plain italic print. If an argument is followed by an ellipsis (...), it is part of a repeatable series (functions can have up to 13 arguments).

See also the FoRmula PasTe Function command.

ABS (*number*)
Returns the absolute value of the *number*.

ACOS (*number*)
Returns the arccosine of the *number*, in radians.

ACOSH (*number*)
Returns the inverse hyperbolic cosine of the *number*.

ADDRESS (*row_num,column_num,*abs_num,a1,sheet_text)
Creates a cell address as text given the row and column numbers.

AND (*logical1,*logical2,...)
Returns TRUE if all arguments are TRUE; otherwise returns FALSE.

AREAS (*reference*)
Returns the number of areas (ranges of contiguous cells or single cells) in the *reference*.

ASIN (*number*)
Returns the arcsine of the *number*, in radians.

ASINH (*number*)
Returns the inverse hyperbolic sine of the *number*.

ATAN (*number*)
Returns the arctangent of the *number*, in radians.

ATAN2 (*x_num,y_num*)
Returns the arctangent of the X and Y coordinates, in radians.

ATANH (*number*)
Returns the inverse hyperbolic tangent of the *number*.

AVERAGE (*number1,*number2,...)
Returns the mean of the *numbers*.

CELL (*info_type,*reference)
Returns information about column width, location, protection, contents, and formatting of the upper-left cell in the *reference*.

CHAR (*number*)

Produces the ANSI character corresponding to the *number* between 1 and 255.

CHOOSE (*index_num,value1,*value2,...)

Returns from the list of arguments the *value* in the position specified by *index_num*.

CLEAN (*text*)

Returns the *text* string with all nonprintable characters removed.

CODE (*text*)

Returns the ANSI code of the first character in the *text* string.

COLUMN (*reference*)

Returns the column number *reference*. If you do not specify any column, returns the column number of the column in which the function appears.

COLUMNS (*array*)

Returns the number of columns in the *array* or reference.

COS (*number*)

Returns the cosine of the *number*.

COSH (*number*)

Returns the hyperbolic cosine of the *number*.

COUNT (*value1,*value2,...)

Counts the numbers in the group of arguments.

COUNTA (*value1,*value2,...)

Counts the number of nonblank *values* in the group of arguments.

DATE (*year,month,day*)

Returns the integer from 1 to 65380 corresponding to the *year*, *month*, and *day* from January 1, 1900, to December 31, 2078.

DATEVALUE (*date_text*)

Returns the integer from 1 to 65380 corresponding to the *date_text* from January 1, 1900, to December 31, 2078.

DAVERAGE (*database,field,criteria*)

Returns the mean of the numbers in the *field* of *database* records that satisfy the *criteria.*

DAY (*serial_number*)

Returns the integer from 1 to 31 that represents the day of the month corresponding to the date from January 1, 1900 and December 31, 2078.

DCOUNT (*database,field,criteria*)

Counts the cells in the *field* of *database* records containing numbers that satisfy the *criteria.* If you do not specify the *field*, Excel counts all nonblank *database* records.

DCOUNTA (*database,field,criteria*)

Counts the nonblank cells in the *field* of *database* records that satisfy the *criteria.*

DDB (*cost,salvage,life,period,factor*)

Calculates depreciation of an asset for the *period* of time based on initial *cost*, *salvage* value, and useful *life*. The balance declines at the rate of *factor*. If you do not specify the *factor*, Excel uses a factor of two.

DGET (*database,field,criteria*)

Extracts the single value that satisfies the *criteria* from the *field* of *database* records.

DMAX (*database,field,criteria*)

Finds largest number in the *field* of *database* records that satisfies the *criteria.*

DMIN (*database,field,criteria*)

Finds smallest number in the *field* of *database* records that satisfies the *criteria.*

DOLLAR (*number,decimals*)

Rounds the *number* to the specified number of *decimals* to the right (for a positive number) or to the left (for a negative number) of the decimal point and converts the *number* to text using currency format. If you do not specify *decimals*, Excel rounds to two places.

DPRODUCT(*database,field,criteria*)

Calculates the product of the numbers in the *field* of *database* records that satisfy the *criteria*.

DSTDEV(*database,field,criteria*)

Approximates the standard deviation based on a sample from the *field* of *database* records that satisfy the *criteria*.

DSTDEVP(*database,field,criteria*)

Calculates the standard deviation based on entire population using numbers from the *field* of *database* records that satisfy the *criteria*.

DSUM(*database,field,criteria*)

Calculates the sum of the numbers in the *field* of *database* records that satisfy the *criteria*.

DVAR(*database,field,criteria*)

Calculates the variance of a population based on a sample from the *field* of *database* records that satisfy the *criteria*.

DVARP(*database,field,criteria*)

Calculates the variance of a population based on the entire population from the *field* of *database* records that satisfy the *criteria*.

EXACT(*text1,text2*)

Returns TRUE if the two *text* strings are identical; otherwise returns FALSE.

EXP(*number*)

Returns e (2.71828182845904) raised to the power of the *number*.

FACT(*number*)

Returns the factorial of the *number*.

FALSE( )

Returns the logical value FALSE.

FIND(*find_text,within_text*,*start_at_num*)

> Returns the integer position at which the *find_text* substring occurs in the *within_text* string. The search begins at 1 or at the *start_at_num* position. This function is case-sensitive and cannot be used with wildcards.

FIXED(*number*,*decimals*)

> Rounds to the specified *number* of *decimal* places and formats with a period and commas and returns the result as text. If you do not specify *decimals*, Excel rounds to two places.

FV(*rate,nper,pmt*,*pv,type*)

> Calculates the future value of an investment based on the constant interest *rate*, the total *number* of periodic payments, the amount of the *payment*, the *present value* of the investment and the *type* of payment arrangement. If you do not specify the *present value* and *type*, Excel considers them to be zero.

GROWTH(*known_y's*,*known_x's,new_x's,const*)

> Calculates Y-values along an exponential curve for the array of new X-values, based on known Y- and X-values. *Const* is a logical value that specifies whether to force the constant to be 1.

HLOOKUP(*lookup_value,table_array,row_index_num*)

> Looks across the top row of the range specified by *table_array* until a match for *lookup_value* is found (if no match is found, Excel uses the largest value less than *lookup_value*), then moves down that column to the row specified by *row_index_num* and returns the contents of that cell.

HOUR(*serial_number*)

> Returns the integer from 0 to 23 that represents the hour (on a 24-hour clock) entered in Excel's *serial_number* or time text format.

IF(*logical_test*,*value_if_true,value_if_false*)

> Returns the *value_if_true* if *logical_test* is TRUE; otherwise, returns the *value_if_false*.

INDEX(*reference,row_num,column_num,area_num*)

Returns the reference of the cell at the intersection of the specified row and column within the *reference*. *Area_num* is used to select a range within the *reference* when multiple ranges are used.

INDEX(*array,row_num,column_num*)

Returns the contents of the cell at the intersection of the specified row and column within the *array*. If the *array* contains only one row or column, the corresponding argument is optional.

INDIRECT(*ref_text,a1*)

Returns the contents of the cell indicated by the contents of another cell. The logical value *a1* specifies the type of reference. If *a1* is TRUE or omitted, the reference is in A1 style; otherwise it is in R1C1 style.

INFO(*type_num*)

Returns information about the current operating environment.

INT(*number*)

Returns the integer resulting from rounding the *number* down.

IPMT(*rate,per,nper,pv,fv,type*)

Calculates the interest payment based on the constant interest *rate*, the payment *period*, the total *number* of constant, periodic payments, the *present value* of the investment, and (optionally) the *future value* and the *type* of payment arrangement.

IRR(*values,guess*)

Calculates the internal rate of return for a series of periodic cash flows. If you do not include a *guess*, Excel uses 10 percent.

ISBLANK(*value*)

Returns TRUE if the argument refers to an empty cell; otherwise returns FALSE.

ISERR(*value*)

> Returns TRUE if the argument is an Excel error *value* other than #N/A (no value available); otherwise returns FALSE.

ISERROR(*value*)

> Returns TRUE if the argument is an Excel error *value*; otherwise returns FALSE.

ISLOGICAL(*value*)

> Returns TRUE if the argument is a logical value; otherwise returns FALSE.

ISNA(*value*)

> Returns TRUE if the argument is the error value #N/A (no value available); otherwise returns FALSE.

ISNONTEXT(*value*)

> Returns TRUE if the argument is not text or a blank cell; otherwise returns FALSE.

ISNUMBER(*value*)

> Returns TRUE if the argument is a number; otherwise returns FALSE.

ISREF(*value*)

> Returns TRUE if the argument is a reference; otherwise returns FALSE.

ISTEXT(*value*)

> Returns TRUE if the argument is text; otherwise returns FALSE.

LEFT(*text*,*num_chars*)

> Returns the leftmost number of characters in a *text* string. If you omit *num_chars*, Excel uses 1.

LEN(*text*)

> Returns the number of characters in the *text*.

LINEST(*known_y's*,*known_x's*,*const*,*stats*)

> Uses the "least-squares" method to calculate the array representing a straight line based on the array of *known_y's* and (optionally) *known_x's*.

LN(*number*)

Calculates the natural logarithm of the positive *number*.

LOG(*number,base*)

Calculates the logarithm of the positive *number* in the specified *base*. If you do not specify the *base*, Excel uses base 10.

LOG10(*number*)

Calculates the logarithm of the positive *number* in base 10.

LOGEST(*known_y's*,*known_x's, const,stats*)

Calculates the horizontal array representing an exponential curve based on the array of *known_y's* and (optionally) *known_x's*.

LOOKUP(*lookup_value,lookup_vector,result_vector*)

Searches the row or column array specified by *lookup_vector* until a match for *lookup_value* is found (if no match is found, Excel uses the largest value less than *lookup_value*), then selects the corresponding position in *result_vector* and returns the contents of that cell. Values must be in ascending order.

LOOKUP(*lookup_value,array*)

Searches the *array's* first column or row until a match for *lookup_value* is found (if no match is found, Excel uses the largest value less than *lookup_value*), then selects the last cell in that row or column and returns the contents of that cell. Values must be in ascending order.

LOWER(*text*)

Converts *text* to lowercase.

MATCH(*lookup_value,lookup_array*,*match_type*)

Returns the position of a match for the value in the array. Selection of the match is based on the following *match_type* codes: if the code is omitted or 1, selects the the largest value less than or equal to the *lookup_value*. If the code is 0, selects the first value equal to *lookup_value*. If the code is -1, selects the smallest value greater than or equal to the *lookup_value*.

MAX(*number1*,*number2*,...)

Returns the largest *number* among the arguments. This function can have up to 14 arguments.

MEDIAN(*number1*,*number2*...)

Returns the median of the *numbers*. This function can have up to 14 arguments.

MID(*text*,*start_num*,*num_chars*)

Returns the substring of *text* that begins at the *start_num* and continues for the *num_chars*.

MIN(*number1*,*number2*,...)

Finds the smallest *number* among the arguments. This function can have up to 14 arguments.

MINUTE(*serial_number*)

Returns the integer from 0 to 59 that represents the minute entered in Excel's *serial_number* or time text format.

MINVERSE(*array*)

Calculates the *array* that is the inverse matrix of the square numeric array.

MIRR(*values*,*finance_rate*,*reinvest_rate*)

Calculates the modified internal rate of return for a series of periodic cash flows. *Values* must contain at least one positive number. *Finance_rate* is the interest rate charged on the money used in the cash flows. *Reinvest_rate* is the interest rate received on the reinvested cash flows.

MMULT(*array1*,*array2*)

Calculates the matrix product of *array1* and *array2*. Both arrays must contain numbers only, and the number of columns and rows must be equal.

MOD(*number*,*divisor*)

Returns the integer remainder that results from dividing the *number* by the *divisor*.

MONTH(*serial_number*)

Returns the integer from 1 to 12 that represents the month entered in Excel's *serial_number* format.

N(*value*)

If the *value* is a number, returns that number. If the *value* is logical TRUE, returns 1. If the *value* is anything else, returns 0.

NA( )

Returns the error value #N/A (no value is available).

NOT(*logical*)

If *logical* is FALSE, returns TRUE. If *logical* is TRUE, returns FALSE.

NOW( )

Returns the *serial_number* for the current date and time in the computer's clock.

NPER(*rate,pmt,pv,fv,type*)

Calculates the number of periods for an investment based on the constant interest *rate*, constant periodic *payments*, the *present value* of the investment, and (optionally) the *future value* and the *type* of payment arrangement.

NPV(*rate,value1,value2,...*)

Calculates the net present value of an investment based on periodic cash flows and the discount *rate*.

OFFSET(*reference,rows,cols,height,width*)

Returns the new reference of the (optional) *height* and *width*, offset from the original *reference* by the number of *rows* and *columns*.

OR(*logical1,logical2,...*)

Returns FALSE if all the arguments are FALSE; otherwise returns TRUE.

PI( )

Returns 3.14159265358979, the mathematical constant π.

PMT(*rate,nper,pv,fv,type*)

Calculates the amount of a single payment for an investment based on the constant interest *rate*, the total *number* of constant periodic payments, the *present value* of the investment, and (optionally) the *future value* and *type* of payment arrangement.

PPMT(*rate,per,nper,pv,fv,type*)

Calculates payment on the principal based on the constant interest *rate*, the *period* of payments, the *number* of constant periodic payments, the *present value* of the investment, and (optionally) the *future value* and *type* of payment arrangement.

PRODUCT(*number1,number2,...*)

Calculates the product of the arguments. This function can have up to 14 arguments.

PROPER(*text*)

Capitalizes the first letter and all letters following non-letter characters. All other letters appear lowercase.

PV(*rate,nper,pmt,fv,type*)

Calculates the present value of an investment based on the constant interest *rate*, the total *number* of constant periodic payments, the amount of a single *payment*, and (optionally) the *future value* of the investment and *type* of payment arrangement.

RAND( )

Returns random number between 0 and 1, including 0 but not 1. Regenerates each time Excel calculates the worksheet.

RATE(*nper,pmt,pv,fv,type,guess*)

Calculates interest rate per period based on the total *number* of constant periodic payments, the amount of a single *payment*, the *present value* of the investment, and, (optionally) the *future value,* the *type* of payment arrangement, and your *guess* of the rate to ensure that RATE iterations converge. If you do not specify a *guess*, Excel uses 10 percent.

REPLACE(*old_text,start_num,num_chars,new_text*)

Replaces the *old_text* substring with the *new_text* substring, beginning at *start_num* and continuing for *num_chars*.

REPT(*text,number_times*)

Repeats the *text* string for the *number of times*.

RIGHT(*text*,*num_chars*)

Returns the text of the rightmost number of characters of the *text* string. If you do not specify *num_chars*, Excel uses 1.

ROUND(*number,num_digits*)

Rounds the number to the number of digits.

ROW(*reference*)

Returns the row number(s) of the row or range of rows. If you do not specify the row, Excel uses the row of the function.

ROWS(*array*)

Returns the number of rows in the *array*.

SEARCH(*find_text*,*within_text*,*start_num*)

Returns the integer position at which the *find_text* substring occurs in the *within_text* string. This function is like FIND, except that SEARCH allows wildcards and is not case-sensitive.

SECOND(*serial_number*)

Returns the integer from 0 to 59 representing the second entered in Excel's *serial_number* or time text formats.

SIGN(*number*)

Returns 1 if the *number* is positive, 0 if 0, and −1 if negative.

SIN(*number*)

Returns the sine of the *number*.

SINH(*number*)

Returns the hyperbolic sine of the *number*.

SLN(*cost,salvage,life*)

Calculates the straight-line depreciation for an asset for one period.

SQRT(*number*)

Calculates the square root of the positive *number*.

STDEV(*number1*,*number2*,...)
> Calculates the standard deviation of a sample population. This function can have up to 14 arguments.

STDEVP(*number1*,*number2*,...)
> Calculates the standard deviation of the entire population. This function can have up to 14 arguments.

SUBSTITUTE(*text*,*old_text*,*new_text*,*instance_number*)
> Substitutes the *new_text* substring for the *old_text* substring. You also can specify the number of times the substring is replaced.

SUM(*number1*,*number2*,...)
> Sums up to 14 *numbers*. Arguments can contain empty cells, logical values, ranges, and numbers in text format.

SUMPRODUCT(*array1*,*array2*,...)
> Multiplies corresponding components in the given arrays and returns the sum of the products.

SYD(*cost*,*salvage*,*life*,*per*)
> Uses the sum-of-the-years method to calculate depreciation of an asset for the *period*, based on the initial *cost*, *salvage* value, and useful *life* of the asset.

T(*value*)
> Returns the text if the *value* is text or a reference to a cell containing text; otherwise returns empty text ("").

TAN(*number*)
> Returns the tangent of the *number*.

TEXT(*value*,*format_text*)
> Converts the *value* to the text format.

TIME(*hour*,*minute*,*second*)
> Returns the *serial_number* (a decimal fraction from 0 to .9999) for the time entered in *hour,minute, second* format.

TIMEVALUE(*time_text*)
> Returns the serial number (a decimal fraction from 0 to .9999) for the time entered in *time_text* format.

TODAY( )

Returns the serial number of the current date in the computer's clock.

TRANSPOSE(*array*)

Transposes the contents of the square *array's* rows and columns.

TREND(*known_y's*,*known_x's*,*new_x's*,*const*)

Uses the "least-squares" method to calculate Y-values along the straight line for the array of new X-values, based on known Y- and X-values. *Const* is a logical value that specifies whether to force to constant to be zero.

TRIM(*text*)

Removes all spaces from the *text* string except for single spaces between words.

TRUE( )

Returns the logical value TRUE.

TRUNC(*number*,*num_digits*)

Truncates the *number* the number of digits after the decimal point.

TYPE(*value*)

Returns the number that represents the data type of the *value* : 1=number, 2=text, 4=logical value, 8=formula,16=error value, and 64=array.

UPPER(*text*)

Converts the *text* to uppercase.

VALUE(*text*)

Converts *text* to a number. Include to ensure compatibility with other spreadsheets.

VAR(*number1*,*number2*,...)

Calculates an estimate of the variance of a population based on a sample population. This function can have up to 14 arguments.

VARP(*number1*,*number2*,...)

> Calculates the variance of a population based on the entire population. This function can have up to 14 arguments.

VDB(*cost*,*salvage*,*life*,*start_period*,*end_period*,
factor,*no_switch*)

> Returns the depreciation of an asset for any period specified.

VLOOKUP(*lookup_value*,*table_array*,*col_index_num*)

> Looks down the leftmost column of the *table_array* range until a match for *lookup_value* is found (if none is found, Excel uses the largest value less than *lookup_value*), then moves across that row to the column specified by *col_index_num* and returns the contents of that cell.

WEEKDAY(*serial_number*)

> Returns the integer from 1 to 7 that represents the day of the week from Sunday (1) to Saturday (7) entered in Excel's *serial_number* or date_text format.

YEAR(*serial_number*)

> Returns the integer from 1900 to 2078 that represents the year entered in Excel's *serial_number* or date _text format.

MACRO FUNCTIONS

> This section alphabetically lists and briefly describes all Excel macro functions except those that duplicate worksheet functions.

A1.R1C1(*logical*)

> Duplicates selecting **O**ptions **W**orkspace **R1C1**.

ABSREF(*ref_text*,*reference*)

> Returns the new absolute cell reference or range that results from the combination of the absolute *reference* with the relative reference (in R1C1 format) *ref_text*.

ACTIVATE(*window_text,pane_num*)
    Duplicates pressing **F6**, activating a pane in a window.

ACTIVATE.NEXT( )
    Duplicates pressing **Ctrl+F6**, activating the
    next window.

ACTIVATE.PREV( )
    Duplicates pressing **Shift+Ctrl+F6**, activating the
    preceding window.

ACTIVE.CELL( )
    Returns the active cell reference in external reference
    format. Generally yields the value in a formula
    or function.

ADD.ARROW( )
    Duplicates the **C**hart Add A**R**row command.

ADD.OVERLAY( )
    Duplicates the **C**hart Add **O**verlay command.

ALERT(*message_text,type_num*)
    Displays the *message* in a dialog box and pauses for
    button selection.

ALIGNMENT(*type_num,*wrap*)
ALIGNMENT?(*type_num,wrap*)
    Duplicates the Forma**T A**lignment command.

APP.MAXIMIZE( )
    Duplicates the Control Ma**X**imize command for the
    application window.

APP.MINIMIZE( )
    Duplicates the Control Mi**N**imize command for the
    application window.

APP.MOVE(*x_num,y_num*)
APP.MOVE?(*x_num,y_num*)
    Duplicates the Control **M**ove command for the
    application window.

APP.RESTORE( )

    Duplicates the Control Restore command for the
application window.

APP.SIZE(*x_num,y_num*)

APP.SIZE?(*x_num,y_num*)

    Duplicates the Control Size command for the
application window.

**APPLY.NAMES(*name_array,*ignore,use_rowcol,omit_col,
omit_row,order_num,append_last)**

**APPLY.NAMES?(*name_array,ignore,use_rowcol,omit_col,
omit_row,order_num,append_last*)**

    Duplicates the FoRmula Apply Names command.

APPLY.STYLE(*style_text*)

APPLY.STYLE?(*style_text*)

    Duplicates the FormaT Style command.

AREAS(*reference*)

    Finds the number of areas in the *reference*.

ARGUMENT(*name_text,*data_type_num)

ARGUMENT(*name_text,data_type_num,ref*)

    Describes arguments to use in a function macro by
name, *type*, and location. Function macros can have up
to 13 arguments.

ARRANGE.ALL( )

    Duplicates the Window Arrange All command.

ASSIGN.TO.OBJECT(*macro_ref*)

ASSIGN.TO.OBJECT?(*macro_ref*)

    Duplicates the Macro Assign to Object command.

ATTACH.TEXT(*attach_to_num,series_num,point_num*)

ATTACH.TEXT?(*attach_to_num,series_num,point_num*)

    Duplicates the Chart Attach Text command.

ATTRIBUTES(*comment_text,auto_share*)

ATTRIBUTES?(*comment_text,auto_share*)

    Duplicates the File Object Attributes command when
working with Excel objects in New Wave.

AXES(**x**_*main*,*y*_*main*,*x*_*over*,*y*_*over*)
AXES?(**x**_*main*,*y*_*main*,*x*_*over*,*y*_*over*)
> Duplicates the Chart AXes command for 2-D charts.

AXES(**x**_*main*,*y*_*main*,*z*_*main*)
AXES?(**x**_*main*,*y*_*main*,*z*_*main*)
> Duplicates the Chart AXes command for 3-D charts.

BEEP(*tone_num*)
> Makes the computer "beep" with a tone specified by the *number* (from 1 to 4). If you omit the argument, Excel uses 1. The effect varies with the type of computer; for example, on the IBM PC, all four numbers result in the same sound.

BORDER(*outline,left,right,top,bottom,shade,outline_color, left_color,right_color,top_color,bottom_color*)
BORDER?(*outline,left,right,top,bottom,shade,outline_color, left_color,right_color,top_color,bottom_color*)
> Duplicates the FormaT Border command.

Break( )
> Breaks the macro execution out of a FOR-NEXT or WHILE-NEXT loop and proceeds to the next instruction.

BRING.TO.FRONT( )
> Duplicates the FormaT Bring To FrOnt command.

CALCULATE.DOCUMENT( )
> Duplicates the Options Calculate Document command (a shifted command). Calculates the active document.

CALCULATE.NOW( )
> Duplicates the Options Calculate Now and Chart Calculate Now commands for all open documents.

CALCULATION(***type_num,****iter,max_num,max_change, update,precision,date_1904,calc_save,save_values*)
CALCULATION?(*type_num,iter,max_num,max_change, update,precision,date_1904,calc_save,save_values*)
> Duplicates the Options Calculation command.

CANCEL.COPY ( )
> Duplicates Esc to eliminate the marquee surrounding a cut or copied area.

CELL.PROTECTION (*locked,hidden*)
CELL.PROTECTION? (*locked,hidden*)
> Duplicates the FormaT Cell Protection command.

CHANGE.LINK (*old_text,new_text,type_of_link*)
CHANGE.LINK? (*old_text,new_text,type_of_link*)
> Duplicates selecting File Links and a document, then selecting the Change button and typing the name of another document. The two arguments must be names of linked files enclosed in quotation marks.

CLEAR (*type_num*)
CLEAR? (*type_num*)
> Duplicates the Edit ClEar command.

CLOSE (*save_logical*)
> Duplicates the Control Close command for the active document window.

CLOSE.ALL ( )
> Duplicates the File Close All command (a shifted command).

COLOR.PALETTE (*file_text*)
COLOR.PALETTE? (*file_text*)
> Duplicates selecting a file from the Copy Color From box in the Options Color PalEtte dialog box.

COLUMN.WIDTH
(*width_num,reference,standard,type_num*)
COLUMN.WIDTH?
(*width_num,reference,standard,type_num*)
> Duplicates the FormaT Column Width command.

COMBINATION (*type_num*)
COMBINATION? (*type_num*)
> Duplicates the Gallery ComBination command.

CONSOLIDATE
(*source_refs,function_num,top_row,left_col,
create_links*)
CONSOLIDATE?
(*source_refs,function_num,top_row,left_col,
create_links*)
Duplicates Data CoNsolidate command.

COPY ( )
Duplicates the Edit Copy command.

COPY.CHART (*size_num*)
COPY.CHART? (*size_num*)
Included for compatibility with Macintosh Excel.

COPY.PICTURE (*appearance_num,size_num*)
Duplicates the Edit Copy Picture command
(a shifted command).

CREATE.NAMES (*top,left,bottom,right*)
CREATE.NAMES? (*top,left,bottom,right*)
Duplicates the FoRmula Create Names command.

CREATE.OBJECT (*object_type,ref_1,x_offset1,
y_offset1,ref_2,x_offset2,y_offset2*)
Draws the *object* and returns a value identifying the
object (for lines, rectangles, ovals, arcs, and pictures).

CREATE.OBJECT (*object_type,ref_1,x_offset1,
y_offset1,ref_2,x_offset2,y_offset2,text*)
Draws the *object* and returns a value identifying the
object (for text boxes and buttons).

CREATE.OBJECT (*object_type,ref_1,x_offset1,
y_offset1,ref_2,x_offset2,y_offset2,xy_series*)
Draws the *object* and returns a value identifying the
object (for embedded charts).

CUT ( )
Duplicates the Edit CuT command.

DATA.DELETE ()
DATA.DELETE? ()
>Duplicates the Data Delete command.

DATA.FIND (*logical*)
>Duplicates the Data Find and Data Exit Find commands.

DATA.FIND.NEXT ()
DATA.FIND.PREV ()
>Duplicates selecting the Data Find command and pressing the down- or up-arrow key.

DATA.FORM ()
>Duplicates the Data FOrm command.

DATA.SERIES (*row_col,type,date,step,stop*)
DATA.SERIES? (*row_col,type,date,step,stop*)
>Duplicates the Data SeRies command.

DEFINE.NAME (*name_text,refers_to,macro_type, shortcut_text,hidden*)
DEFINE.NAME? (*name_text,refers_to,macro_type, shortcut_text,hidden*)
>Duplicates the FoRmula Define Name command.

DEFINE.STYLE (*style_text,number,font,alignment,border, pattern,protection*)
DEFINE.STYLE? (*style_text,number,font,alignment,border, pattern,protection*)
>Duplicates selecting the FormaT Style command and choosing the Define button.

DELETE.ARROW ()
>Duplicates the Chart Delete ARrow command.

DELETE.FORMAT (*format_text*)
>Duplicates the FormaT Number command to delete a *format*.

DELETE.NAME (*name_text*)
>Duplicates the FoRmula Define Name command to delete a *name*.

DELETE.OVERLAY ()
>Duplicates the Chart Delete Overlay command.

DELETE.STYLE (*style_text*)

Duplicates selecting the FormaT Style command,then choosing the Delete button.

DEMOTE (*rowcol*)

DEMOTE? (*rowcol*)

Duplicates selecting *rows* or *columns*, then clicking the demote button.

DEREF (*reference*)

Returns the value(s) in the cells you *reference*.

DIRECTORY (*path_text*)

Changes the drive and directory to the path specified by *path_text* and returns the new directory in text format. If you omit *path_text*, returns the current directory.

DISPLAY (*formula,gridlines,headings,zeros,color_num, reserved,outline,page_breaks,object_num*)

DISPLAY? (*formula,gridlines,headings,zeros,color_num, reserved,outline,page_breaks,object_num*)

Duplicates the Options Display command.

DISPLAY (*cell,formula,value,format,protect,names,precedents, dependents,note*)

Duplicates commands from the Info menu.

DOCUMENTS (*type_num*)

Returns a horizontal alphabetical array of the text names of all open documents.

DUPLICATE ( )

Duplicates the selected object.

EDIT.COLOR (*color_num,red_value,green_value,blue_value*)

EDIT.COLOR? (*color_num,red_value,green_value,blue_value*)

Selects new colors for the color palette, assigning the *color_num* from 1 to 16.

EDIT.DELETE (*shift_num*)

EDIT.DELETE? (*shift_num*)

Duplicates the Edit Delete command.

EDIT.REPEAT ( )
>   Duplicates the Edit Repeat command.

EDIT.SERIES (*series_num,name_ref,x_ref,y_ref,z_ref, plot_order*)
EDIT.SERIES? (*series_num,name_ref,x_ref,y_ref,z_ref, plot_order*)
>   Duplicates the Chart Edit Series command.

ELSE ( )
>   Controls the functions used with IF, ELSE.IF, and END.IF.

ELSE.IF (*logical_test*)
>   Controls the functions used with IF, ELSE, and END.IF.

END.IF ( )
>   Ends the block of functions that began with an IF function.

EXTRACT (*unique*)

EXTRACT? (*unique*)
>   Duplicates the Data Extract command.

FILE.CLOSE (*save_logical*)
>   Duplicates the File Close command.

FILE.DELETE (*file_text*)

FILE.DELETE? (*file_text*)
>   Duplicates the File Delete command.

FILES (*directory_text*)
>   Returns a horizontal array of the file names in the *directory*.

FILL.DOWN ( )
>   Duplicates the Edit Fill DoWn command.

FILL.LEFT ( )
>   Duplicates the Edit Fill Left (H) command (a shifted command).

FILL.RIGHT ( )
>   Duplicates the Edit Fill Right command.

FILL.UP ( )
> Duplicates the Edit Fill Up (W) command
> (a shifted command).

FILL.WORKGROUP (*type_num*)
FILL.WORKGROUP? (*type_num*)
> Duplicates the Edit Fill WorkGroup command.

FONT (*name_text,size_num*)
FONT? (*name_text,size_num*)
> Included for compatibility with Macintosh Excel.

FOR (*counter_text,start_num,end_num,step_num*)
> Executes in a loop all instructions between the macro
> and a NEXT statement until *counter_text* exceeds
> *end_num*.

FOR.CELL (*ref_name,area_ref,skip_blanks*)
> Starts a FOR.CELL-NEXT loop.

FORMAT.FONT (*name_text,size_num,bold,italic,underline,
strike,color,outline,shadow*)
FORMAT.FONT?
(*name_text,size_num,bold,italic,underline,
strike,color,outline,shadow*)
> Duplicates the Format Font command for cells of a
> worksheet or macro sheet.

FORMAT.FONT (*name_text,size_num,bold,italic,underline,
strike,color,outline,shadow,object_id_text,start_num,char_num*)
FORMAT.FONT?
(*name_text,size_num,bold,italic,underline,
strike,color,outline,shadow,object_id_text,start_num,char_num*)
> Duplicates the Format Font command for text boxes and
> buttons on a worksheet or macro sheet.

FORMAT.FONT (*color,backgd,apply,name,name_text,size,
bold,italic,underline,strike,outline,shadow*)
FORMAT.FONT? (*color,backgd,apply,name,name_text,size,
bold,italic,underline,strike,outline,shadow*)
> Duplicates the Format Font command for chart items.

FORMAT.LEGEND (*position_num*)

FORMAT.LEGEND? (*position_num*)
> Duplicates the Format Legend command.

FORMAT.MAIN (*type_num,*view,overlap,gap_width,vary,
drop,hilo,angle,gap_depth,chart_depth)
**FORMAT.MAIN? (*type_num,view,overlap,gap_width,vary,*
drop,hilo,angle,gap_depth,chart_depth)**
> Duplicates the FormaT Main Chart command.

FORMAT.MOVE (*x_offset,y_offset,*reference)

FORMAT.MOVE? (*x_offset,y_offset,reference*)
> Duplicates the Format Move command for worksheet
> objects.

FORMAT.MOVE (*x_pos,y_pos*)

FORMAT.MOVE? (*x_pos,y_pos*)
> Duplicates the Format Move command for chart objects.

FORMAT.NUMBER (*format_text*)

FORMAT.NUMBER? (*format_text*)
> Duplicates the Format Number command.

FORMAT.OVERLAY (*type_num,*view,overlap,width,vary,
drop,hilo,angle,series_dist,series_num)
**FORMAT.OVERLAY? (*type_num,view,overlap,width,vary,*
drop,hilo,angle,series_dist,series_num)**
> Duplicates the FormaT Overlay command.

FORMAT.SIZE (*width,height*)
FORMAT.SIZE? (*width,height*)
> Duplicates the Format Size command (for absolute
> worksheet objects and chart items).

FORMAT.SIZE (*x_off,y_off,*reference)

FORMAT.SIZE? (*x_off,y_off,*reference)
> Duplicates the Format Size command (for relative
> worksheet objects).

**FORMAT.TEXT (*x_align,y_align,orient_num,auto_text,*
auto_size,show_key,show_value)**

FORMAT.TEXT? (*x_align,y_align,orient_num,auto_text, auto_size,show_key,show_value*)

Duplicates the Format Text command.

FORMULA (*formula_text,reference*)

If the active document is a worksheet, duplicates entering the *formula* in a cell. If you omit the *reference*, Excel uses the active cell. If the active document is a chart, duplicates entering text labels or SERIES formulas.

FORMULA.ARRAY (*formula_text,reference*)

Duplicates pressing Ctrl+Shift+Enter to enter an array *formula*. If you omit the *reference*, Excel uses the current selection.

FORMULA.CONVERT (*formula_text,from_a1,to_a1, to_ref_type,rel_to_ref*)

Converts formulas in quoted text form by changing R1C1 style and absolute/relative reference.

FORMULA.FILL (*formula_text,reference*)

Duplicates pressing Ctrl to enter a formula. If you omit the *reference*, Excel uses the current selection.

FORMULA.FIND (*text,in_num,at_num,by_num,dir_num, match_case*)

FORMULA.FIND? (*text,in_num,at_num,by_num,dir_num, match_case*)

Duplicates the FoRmula Find command.

FORMULA.FIND.NEXT ()

FORMULA.FIND.PREV ()

Duplicates pressing F7 and Shift+F7, respectively. Finds next and preceding occurrences of the value in the FoRmula Find dialog box.

FORMULA.GOTO (*reference,corner*)

FORMULA.GOTO? (*reference,corner*)

Duplicates selecting the Formula Goto command or pressing F5.

FORMULA.REPLACE (*find_text,replace_text,look_at, look_by, active_cell,match_case*)

FORMULA.REPLACE? (*find_text,replace_text,look_at,*
look_by,active_cell,match_case)
    Duplicates the Formula REplace command.

FREEZE.PANES (*logical*)
    Duplicates the Options Freeze Panes command if
    argument is TRUE; otherwise duplicates the Options
    UnFreeze Panes command.

FULL (*logical*)
    If *logical* is TRUE, duplicates selecting Control
    MaXimize for the active document window. If *logical* is
    FALSE, duplicates selecting Control Restore to restore
    the window to its preceding size.

GALLERY.3D.AREA (*type_num*)
GALLERY.3D.AREA? (*type_num*)
    Duplicates the Gallery 3-D ArEa command.

GALLERY.3D.COLUMN (*type_num*)
GALLERY.3D.COLUMN? (*type_num*)
    Duplicates the Gallery 3-D COlumn command.

GALLERY.3D.LINE (*type_num*)
GALLERY.3D.LINE? (*type_num*)
    Duplicates the Gallery 3-D LiNe command.

GALLERY.3D.PIE (*type_num*)
GALLERY.3D.PIE? (*type_num*)
    Duplicates the Gallery 3-D PIe command.

GALLERY.AREA (*type_num,delete_overlay*)
GALLERY.AREA? (*number,delete_overlay*)
    Duplicates the Gallery Area command.

GALLERY.BAR (*type_num,delete_overlay*)
GALLERY.BAR? (*number,delete_overlay*)
    Duplicates the Gallery Bar command.

GALLERY.COLUMN (*type_num,delete_overlay*)
GALLERY.COLUMN? (*number,delete_overlay*)
    Duplicates the Gallery Column command.

GALLERY.LINE (*type_num,delete_overlay*)

GALLERY.LINE? (*number,delete_overlay*)
Duplicates the Gallery Line command.

GALLERY.PIE (*type_num,delete_overlay*)

GALLERY.PIE? (*number,delete_overlay*)
Duplicates the Gallery Pie command.

GALLERY.SCATTER (*type_num,delete_overlay*)

GALLERY.SCATTER? (*number,delete_overlay*)
Duplicates the Gallery Scatter command.

GET.CELL (*type_num,reference*)
Returns a variety of information about the contents,
formatting, and location of the first cell in the *reference*.
if you omit *reference*, Excel uses the current selection.
Forty *type_num* codes exist.

GET.CHART.ITEM (*x_y_index,point_index,item_text*)
Returns the horizontal or vertical position of the *point* on
the chart *item*.

GET.DEF (*def_text,document_text,type_num*)
Returns the range name for the specified reference in
the *document*.

GET.DOCUMENT (*type_num,name_text*)
Returns a variety of information about the specified
document. If you omit *name_text*, Excel uses the active
document. Forty-four *type_num* codes exist.

GET.FORMULA (*reference*)
Returns the contents of the first cell in the *reference* in
text format.

GET.LINK.INFO

(*link_text,type_num,type_of_link,reference*)
Returns information about the update settings for
the *link*.

GET.NAME (*name_text*)
Returns the definition of the specified range. Duplicates
the Refers To text box for the Formula Define Name
command.

GET.NOTE (*cell_ref,start_char,num_char*)

> Returns the substring of the note attached to *cell_ref*. If you omit *start_char*, Excel uses 1. If you omit *num_char*, Excel returns the rest of the note.

GET.OBJECT

(*type_num*,*object_id,_text,start_num,count_num*)

> Returns information about the *object*. Forty *type_num* codes exist.

GET.WINDOW (***type_num*,*window_text*)**

> Returns a variety of information about the *window*. If you omit *name_text*, Excel uses the active window. Twenty-two *type_num* codes exist.

GET.WORKSPACE (***type_num*)**

> Returns a variety of information about the workspace. Twenty-nine *type_num* codes exist.

GOAL.SEEK (***target_cell,target_value,variable_cell*)**

GOAL.SEEK? (*target_cell,target_value,variable_cell*)

> Duplicates the FoRmula GoaL Seek command.

GOTO (***reference*)**

> Transfers macro execution to the upper left cell in the *reference*.

GRIDLINE(*x*_major,x_minor,y_major,y_minor,z_major, z_minor)

GRIDLINES? (*x_major,x_minor,y_major,y_minor,z_major, z_minor*)

> Duplicates the Chart Gridlines command.

GROUP ()

> Duplicates the FormaT Group command.

HIDE ()

> Duplicates the Window Hide command.

HIDE.OBJECT (*object_id_text,hide*)

> Hides or displays the specified object.

HLINE (***num_columns*)**

> Horizontally scrolls the active window right by the *number of columns*. If the number is negative, scrolls left rather than right.

HPAGE (*num_windows*)

Horizontally scrolls the active window right by the
number of window widths. If the number is negative,
scrolls left rather than right.

HSCROLL (*position,*col_logical*)

If *col_logical* is TRUE, scrolls to column *position*;
otherwise, scrolls to the column that is *position* percent
away from the leftmost edge of the document.

IF (*logical_test*)

Used with ELSE, ELSE.IF, and END.IF to control
execution of formulas on a macro sheet.

**INPUT (*message_text,*type_num,title_text,default,x_pos,*
y_pos)**

Shows a dialog box and returns the data that you enter in
the box.

INSERT (*shift_num*)

INSERT? (*shift_num*)

Duplicates the Edit Insert command.

JUSTIFY ()

Duplicates the FoRmat Justify command.

LAST.ERROR ()

Returns the reference of the last error in the macro sheet.

LEGEND (*logical*)

Duplicates the Chart Add Legend command if argument
is TRUE; otherwise, deletes the legend.

LINKS (*document_text,type_num*)

Returns a horizontal array of the names of worksheets
linked by external references in the *document*.

LIST.NAMES ()

Duplicates selecting the FoRmula Paste Name command
and choosing the Paste List button.

**MAIN.CHART (*type_num,*stack,100,vary,overlap,drop,*
hilo,overlap%,cluster,angle)**

MAIN.CHART? (*type_num*,*stack,100,vary,overlap,drop,*
hilo,overlap%,cluster,angle)

>   Duplicates the FoRmat Main Chart command used in
>   Excel version 2.2 or earlier.

MAIN.CHART.TYPE (*type*)

>   Included for compatibility with Macintosh Excel
>   (version 1.5 or earlier).

MERGE.STYLES (*document_text*)

>   Duplicates selecting the FormaT Style command and
>   choosing the Merge button

MESSAGE (*logical,text*)

>   If *logical* is TRUE, displays the *text* in the message area
>   of the status bar. If *logical* is FALSE, removes all
>   messages from the status bar, and returns the status bar
>   to normal.

MOVE (*x_pos,y_pos,window_text*)

MOVE? (*x_pos,y_pos,window_text*)

>   Duplicates the Control Move command.

NAMES (*document_text,type_num*)

>   Returns a horizontal text array of all names defined in
>   the *document.* If you omit *document_text,* Excel uses the
>   active document.

NEW (*type_num*,*xy_series*)

NEW? (*type_num,xy_series*)

>   Duplicates the File New command.

NEW.WINDOW ( )

>   Duplicates the Window New Window command.

NEXT ( )

>   Defines the end of a FOR-NEXT or WHILE-NEXT
>   loop.

NOT (*logical*)

>   Reverses the value of its argument.

NOTE (*add_text,cell_ref,start_char,num_chars*)

NOTE? ()

> Duplicates the FoRmula Note command. Starting at the specified position in the note attached to the specified cell, replaces the number of characters with new text.

OBJECT.PROTECTION (*locked,lock_text*)
Duplicates the FormaT ProtectIon command.

OFFSET (***reference,rows,cols,****height,width*)

> Offsets the cell reference or range specified by *ref* by a specified number of *rows* and *columns*, then returns the resulting reference. The *height* and *width* of the reference also can be specified.

OPEN (***file_text,****update_links,read_only,format,prot_pwd,*
write_res_pwd,ignore_rorec,file_origin)
OPEN? (*file_text,update_links,read_only,format,prot_pwd,*
write_res_pwd,ignore_rorec,file_origin)
Duplicates the File Open command.

OPEN.LINKS (***doc_text1,****doc_text2,...,read_only,*
type_of_link)
OPEN.LINKS? (***doc_text1,****doc_text2,...,read_only,*
type_of_link)
Duplicates the File Links command.

OUTLINE (*auto_styles,row_dir,col_dir,create_apply*)
Duplicates the FoRmula Outline command.

OVERLAY (***type_num,****stack,100,vary,overlap,drop,hilo,*
overlap%,cluster, angle,series_num,auto)
OVERLAY (*type_num,stack,100,vary,overlap,drop,hilo,*
overlap%,cluster,angle,series_num,auto)
Duplicates the FoRmat Overlay command.

OVERLAY.CHART.TYPE (***type_num***)

> Included for compatibility with Macintosh Excel (version 1.5 or earlier).

PAGE.SETUP (*head,foot,left,right,top,bot,heading,grid,*
h_cent,v_cent,orientation,paper_size,scaling)
PAGE.SETUP? (*head,foot,left,right,top,bot,heading,grid,*
h_cent,v_cent,orientation,paper_size,scaling)
Duplicates the File Page SeTup command for worksheets and macro sheets.

PAGE.SETUP (*head,foot,left,right,top,bot,size,h_cent,v_cent,*
orientation,paper_size,scaling)
PAGE.SETUP?
(*head,foot,left,right,top,bot,size,h_cent,v_cent,*
orientation,paper_size,scaling)
    Duplicates the File Page SeTup command for charts.

PARSE (*text*)
PARSE? (*text*)
    Duplicates the Data Parse command.

PASTE ()
    Duplicates the Edit Paste command.

PASTE.LINK ()
    Duplicates the Edit Paste Link command.

PASTE.PICTURE ()
    Duplicates the Edit Paste Picture command.

PASTE.PICTURE.LINK ()
    Duplicates selecting the Edit Paste Picture Link
    command or using the camera tool.

PASTE.SPECIAL (*paste_num,operation_num,skip_blanks,*
transpose)
PASTE.SPECIAL? (*paste_num,operation_num,skip_blanks,*
transpose)
    Duplicates the Edit Paste Special command for pasting
    from a worksheet or macro sheet into a worksheet or
    macro sheet.

PASTE.SPECIAL (*rowcol,series,categories,replace*)
PASTE.SPECIAL? (*rowcol,series,categories,replace*)
    Duplicates the Edit Paste Special command for pasting
    from a worksheet into a chart.

PASTE.SPECIAL (*paste_num*)
PASTE.SPECIAL? (*paste_num*)
    Duplicates the Edit Paste Special command for pasting
    from one chart into another chart.

PATTERNS (*apattern,afore,aback*)

PATTERNS? (*apattern,afore,aback*)
>   Duplicates the FormaT Patterns command (for cells).

PATTERNS (*lauto,lstyle,lcolor,lwt,hwidth,hlength,htype*)
PATTERNS? (*lauto,lstyle,lcolor,lwt,hwidth,hlength,htype*)
>   Duplicates the FormaT Patterns command (for lines).

PATTERNS (*bauto,bstyle,bcolor,bwt,shadow,aauto,apattern,
afore,aback,rounded*)
PATTERNS?
(*bauto,bstyle,bcolor,bwt,shadow,aauto,apattern,
afore,aback,rounded*)
>   Duplicates the FormaT Patterns command (for text
>   boxes, rectangles, ovals, arcs, and pictures).

PATTERNS (*bauto,bstyle,bcolor,bwt,shadow,aauto,apattern,
afore,aback,invert,apply*)
PATTERNS?
(*bauto,bstyle,bcolor,bwt,shadow,aauto,apattern,
afore,aback,invert,apply*)
>   Duplicates the FormaT Patterns command (for chart plot
>   areas, bars, columns, pie slices, and text labels).

PATTERNS (*lauto,lstyle,lcolor,lwt,tmajor,tminor,tlabel*)
PATTERNS? (*lauto,lstyle,lcolor,lwt,tmajor,tminor,tlabel*)
>   Duplicates the FormaT Patterns command (for
>   chart axes).

PATTERNS (*lauto,lstyle,lcolor,lwt,apply*)
PATTERNS? (*lauto,lstyle,lcolor,lwt,apply*)
>   Duplicates the FormaT Patterns command
>   (for chart lines).

PATTERNS (*lauto,lstyle,lcolor,lwt,mauto,mstyle,mfore,
mback,apply*)
PATTERNS? (*lauto,lstyle,lcolor,lwt,mauto,mstyle,mfore,
mback,apply*)
>   Duplicates the FormaT Patterns command (for
>   chart data lines).

PATTERNS (*type,picture_units,apply*)
PATTERNS? (*type,picture_units,apply*)
>   Duplicates the FormaT Patterns command (for
>   picture chart markers).

PLACEMENT (*placement_type*)

Duplicates the FormaT Object PLacement command.

PRECISION (***logical***)

Duplicates selecting the Options Calculation command and setting the Precision as Displayed check box (TRUE argument turns off the box; FALSE turns on the box).

PREFERRED ( )

Duplicates the Gallery PReferred command.

PRINT (*range_num,from,to,copies,draft,preview,print_what, color,feed*)
PRINT?
(*range_num,from,to,copies,draft,preview,print_what, color,feed*)

Duplicates the File Print command.

PRINT.PREVIEW ( )

Duplicates the File Print PreView command.

PRINTER.SETUP (***printer_text***)
PRINTER.SETUP? (*printer_text*)

Duplicates the File PRinter Setup command.

PROMOTE (*rowcol*)
PROMOTE? (*rowcol*)

Duplicates clicking the outline promote button on the tool bar.

PROTECT.DOCUMENT (*contents,windows,password, objects*)
PROTECT.DOCUMENT? (*contents,windows,password, objects*)

If the active document is a worksheet or macro sheet, duplicates the Options Protect Document (when *contents*, *windows*, or *objects* are TRUE) and Options Unprotect Document (when *contents*, *windows*, or *objects* are FALSE) commands. If the active document is a chart, duplicates the Chart Protect Document (when either or both arguments are TRUE) and Chart UnProtect Document (when both arguments are FALSE) commands.

QUIT ()

Duplicates the File EXit command.

REFTEXT (*reference,a1*)

Converts a reference to an absolute reference in text format.

RELREF (*reference,rel_to_ref*)

Returns in R1C1 format the relative location of the *reference* with respect to the upper left cell of the *rel_to_ref*.

REMOVE.PAGE.BREAK ()

Duplicates the Options Remove Page Break command.

REPLACE.FONT (*font_num,name_text,size_num,bold, italic,underline,strike,color,outline,shadow*)

Duplicates selecting Format Font, then a font number, the Font button, a new font, and the Replace button.

ROW.HEIGHT (*height_num,reference,standard_height, type_num*)

ROW.HEIGHT? (*height_num,reference,standard_height, type_num*)

Duplicates the FoRmat Row Height command.

RUN (*reference,step*)

RUN? (*reference,step*)

Duplicates the Macro Run command.

SAVE ()

Duplicates the File Save command.

SAVE.AS (*document_text,type_num,prot_pwd,backup, write_res_pwd,read_only_rec*)

SAVE.AS? (*document_text,type_num,prot_pwd,backup, write_res_pwd,read_only_rec*)

Duplicates the File Save As command.

SAVE.NEW.OBJECT (*object_name*)

SAVE.NEW.OBJECT? (*object_name*)

Duplicates File Save New Object command when working with Excel objects in New Wave.

SAVE.WORKSPACE (*name_text*)

SAVE.WORKSPACE? (*name_text*)

Duplicates the **F**ile **S**ave **W**orkspace command.

SCALE (*cross,cat_labels,cat_marks,between,max,reverse*)

SCALE? (*cross,cat_labels,cat_marks,between,max,reverse*)

Duplicates the Fo**R**mat **S**cale command.for a 2-D chart's X-axis.

SCALE (*min_num,max_num,major,minor,cross,logarithmic, reverse,max*)

SCALE? (*min_num,max_num,major,minor,cross,logarithmic, reverse,max*)

Duplicates the Fo**R**mat **S**cale command for a 2-D chart's Y-axis or for an XY Scatter chart's X or Y axis.

SCALE (*cat_labels,cat_marks,reverse,between*)

Duplicates the Fo**R**mat **S**cale command.for a 3-D chart's X-axis.

SCALE (*series_labels,series_marks,reverse*)

Duplicates the Fo**R**mat **S**cale command for a 3-D chart's Y-axis.

SCAL (*min_num,max_num,major,minor,cross,logarithmic, reverse,min*)

Duplicates the Fo**R**mat **S**cale command for a 3-D chart's Z-axis.

SELECT (*object_id_text,replace*)

Duplicates selecting the *object* on a worksheet or macro sheet.

SELECT (*selection,active_cell*)

Selects cells or changes the *active cell*. For worksheets and macro sheets only.

SELECT (*item_text,single_point*)

Selects a chart object based on one of twenty-nine *item_text* codes. For charts only.

SELECT.CHART ()

Included for compatibility with Macintosh Excel.

SELECT.END (*direction_num*)

Duplicates pressing **Ctrl-** an arrow key. Activates the cell at the next block edge in specified direction (1=Left, 2=Right, 3=Up, 4=Down).

SELECT.LAST.CELL ()

Duplicates selecting Fo**R**mula **S**elect Special and choosing the Last Cell option.

SELECT.PLOT.AREA ()

Included for compatibility with Macintosh Excel.

SELECT.SPECIAL (*type_num,value_type,levels*)
SELECT.SPECIAL? (*type_num,value_type,levels*)

Duplicates the Fo**R**mula **S**elect Special command.

SELECTION ()

Returns the reference of the current selection as an external reference. Generally yields the value in a function or operation.

SEND.TO.BACK ()

Duplicates the Forma**T** S**E**nd To Back command.

SET.CRITERIA ()

Duplicates the **D**ata Set **C**riteria command.

SET.DATABASE ()

Duplicates the **D**ata Set Data**B**ase command.

SET.EXTRACT ()

Duplicates the **D**ata Set E**X**tract command.

SET.PAGE.BREAK ()

Duplicates the **O**ptions Set Page **B**reak command.

SET.PREFERRED ()

Duplicates the **G**allery Se**T** Preferred command.

SET.PRINT.AREA ()

Duplicates the **O**ptions Set Print **A**rea command.

SET.PRINT.TITLES ()

Duplicates the **O**ptions Set Print **T**itles command.

SET.UPDATE.STATUS (*link_text,status,type_of_link*)

Changes the update *status* to automatic or manual.

SHORT.MENUS (*logical*)

Duplicates the Options Short Menus (when argument is TRUE) and Options Full Menus (when argument is FALSE) commands or the Chart Short Menus (when argument is TRUE) and Chart Full Menus (when argument is FALSE) commands.

SHOW.ACTIVE.CELL ( )

Duplicates the FoRmula SHow Active Cell command. Moves the active cell into view in the current window.

SHOW.CLIPBOARD ( )

Duplicates running the Clipboard application from the Application Control menu.

SHOW.DETAIL (*rowcol,rowcol_num,expand*)

Expands or collapses detail in an outline.

SHOW.INFO (*logical*)

Duplicates the Window Show Info (if *logical* is TRUE) and Window Show Document (if Info window is active and *logical* is FALSE) commands.

SHOW.LEVELS (*row_level,col_level*)

Displays *row* or *column levels* in an outline.

SIZE (*width,height,window_text*)

Duplicates the Control SiZe command for the document window.

SORT (*sort_by,key1,order1,key2,order2,key3,order3*)
SORT? (*sort_by,key1,order1,key2,order2,key3,order3*)

Duplicates the Data Sort command.

SPLIT (*col_split,row_split*)

Duplicates the Control Split command for the document window.

STANDARD.FONT
(*font_text,size_num,bold,italic,underline,*
strike,color,outline,shadow*)

Defines the Standard font style for the active worksheet or macro sheet.

STEP ()
> Initiates single-stepping macro execution (useful for debugging).

STYLE (*bold,italic*)
STYLE? (*bold,italic*)
> Included for compatibility with Macintosh Excel (version 1.5 or earlier).

TABLE (*row_ref,column_ref*)
TABLE? (*row_ref,column_ref*)
> Duplicates the Data Table command.

TEXTREF (*text,a1*)
> Converts the *text* into a reference.

UNDO ()
> Duplicates the Edit Undo command.

UNGROUP ()
> Duplicates the FormaT UnGroup command.

UNHIDE (*window_text*)
> Duplicates the Window UnHide command.

UNLOCKED.NEXT ()
UNLOCKED.PREV ()
> Duplicates pressing Tab or Shift+Tab to activate the next or preceding unlocked cell in a worksheet that is protected.

UPDATE.LINK (*link_text,type_of_link*)
> Duplicates selecting the File Links command and choosing the Update button.

VIEW.3D (*elevation,perspective,rotation,axes,height%*)
VIEW.3D? (*elevation,perspective,rotation,axes,height%*)
> Duplicates the FormaT 3-D View command

VLINE (*num_rows*)
> Vertically scrolls down the active window by the *number of rows*. If *number_rows* is negative, scrolls up rather than down.

VPAGE (*num_windows*)

Vertically scrolls down the active window by the *number of windows*. If *number_windows* is negative, scrolls up rather than down.

VSCROLL (*position,*row_logical)

If *row_logical* is TRUE, scrolls to row *position*; otherwise, scrolls to the row that is *position* percent away from the top of the window.

WAIT (*serial_number*)

Pauses a macro until the time specified by the *serial_number*.

WHILE (*logical_test*)

Executes in a loop all instructions between this function and a NEXT statement until the argument is FALSE.

WINDOWS (*type_num*)

Returns a horizontal text array of the names of all windows on-screen.

WORKGROUP (*name_array*)

Duplicates the Window Workgroup command.

WORKSPACE (*fixed,decimals,r1c1,scroll,status,formula, menu_key,remote,entermove,underines,tools,notes,nav_keys, menu_key_action*)

WORKSPACE? (*fixed,decimals,r1c1,scroll,status,formula, menu_key,remote,entermove,underines,tools,notes,nav_keys, menu_key_action*)

Duplicates the Options Workspace command.

MACRO KEY CODES

To represent most characters in a macro, you type the character as it appears on-screen. Some keyboard keys, however, do not display a character when the key is pressed. For these keys, type the following codes:

Key	*Code*
Backspace	{BACKSPACE} or {BS}
Break	{BREAK}
Caps Lock	{CAPSLOCK}
Clear	{CLEAR}
Del	{DELETE} or {DEL}
Down	{DOWN}
End	{END}
Enter	{ENTER}
Esc	{ESCAPE} or {ESC}
Help	{HELP}
Home	{HOME}
Ins	{INSERT}
Left	{LEFT}
Num Lock	{NUMLOCK}
PgDn	{PGDN}
PgUp	{PGUP}
Prtsc	{PRTSC}
Return	{RETURN} or ~ (tilde)
Right	{RIGHT}
Scroll Lock	{SCROLLLOCK}
Tab	{TAB}
Up	{UP}
F1	{F1}
F2	{F2}
F3	{F3}
F4	{F4}
F5	{F5}
F6	{F6}

F7	{F7}
F8	{F8}
F9	{F9}
F10	{F10}
F11	{F11}
F12	{F12}
F13	{F13}
F14	{F14}
F15	{F15}
F16	{F16}

You also can specify keys combinations. To combine a key with **Shift**, use a plus sign (+). To combine a key with **Ctrl**, use a caret (^). To combine a key with **Alt**, use a percent sign (%). To combine a key with **Command**, use an asterisk (*).

Index

U-Z